BODY SHAPING WITH *Free Weights*

EASY ROUTINES FOR YOUR HOME WORKOUT

Stephenie Karony
&
Anthony L. Ranken

Sterling Publishing Co., Inc.
New York

Edited by Claire Bazinet

10 9 8 7 6 5 4 3 2 1

Published by Sterling Publishing Company, Inc.
387 Park Avenue South, New York, N.Y. 10016

Distributed in Canada by Sterling Publishing
c/o Canadian Manda Group, One Atlantic Avenue, Suite 105
Toronto, Ontario, Canada M6K 3E7
Distributed in Great Britain and Europe by Cassell PLC
Wellington House, 125 Strand, London WC2R 0BB, England
Distributed in Australia by Capricorn Link (Australia) Pty Ltd.
P.O. Box 6651, Baulkham Hills, Business Centre, NSW 2153, Australia
Manufactured in the United States of America

Sterling ISBN 0-8069-9474-6

Contents

Introduction

What Is Body Shaping?

So you really want to change the shape of your body? Lift weights! Working out with weights, or "resistance training," builds a better physique and a healthier body. Resistance training can tighten and tone your muscles, increase your size by adding inches where you want them, and help you control your weight so you can lose inches where you don't want them.

In short, lifting weights is the most effective and the quickest way to create a positive change in the shape of your body. If you follow the advice in this book, you'll see visible results within a few months of beginning a regular exercise program. Stick with it, and you'll just keep getting better.

Women often don't want to train with weights because they are afraid they'll bulk up. In fact, because women don't have high levels of muscle-building hormones, they will find it *very hard* to add on enough muscle mass to look bulky.

The method of training required to develop bulky muscles is called "bodybuilding." This book focuses primarily on "body shaping," or "body sculpting." The exercises are basically the same, but the training methods are different. Body shaping requires less time and lighter weights than a bodybuilding training regimen. The typical bodybuilder trains 6 or even 7 days a week, a couple of hours each day. Body shaping is much less time and energy intensive—you can develop a great shape by training 3 to 4 times a week for 45 minutes to an hour each time. And, if your definition of a well-shaped body includes big muscles, we'll show you how to achieve that, too!

Aside from the time invested, diet is probably the biggest difference between these two training camps. Bodybuilders' diets are very strict and very limited. What and when they eat has evolved into an exact science. Such a diet is not recommended for the person who works out with weights only in order to be shapely and healthy. In Chapter 3 of this book, we'll show you how to eat for greater energy, good health, and a great working body—without the extreme dietary sacrifices that bodybuilders make.

Another big difference between these two methods of training is that bodybuilders usually train with a particular event or goal in mind, whereas body shaping with free weights is about being healthy and having a strong, attractive body over the long term.

What Are Free Weights?

Free weights fall into three categories: barbells, dumbbells, and weight-stack equipment, where gravity is the source of resistance. Once you learn the proper use of the three types of equipment, correct lifting techniques, and some basic exercise theory, free weights will build a strong and shapely body faster and better than any other method of working out.

There are several brands of resistance-training machines available now in gyms and for home use. How do these compare with free weights? For one thing, exercising with free weights more effectively duplicates how human beings move naturally. With free weights, more

Gym equipment used in conjunction with free weights allows the maximum variety in training.

muscles are involved, as one balances and stabilizes the weights. This effort targets not just the "prime mover" in a given exercise, but also the smaller accessory muscles. Even the lifting of weights off their rack requires a wide range of balancing and stabilizing actions. Working out with dumbbells and barbells takes greater effort, and gives you a more complete workout. Machines stabilize the weights for you, so balance and coordination are not enhanced and accessory muscles are not involved.

When you lift a barbell or dumbbell, the resistance is greater at the beginning of the movement; then, to some extent momentum helps with the rest of the movement. Think of lifting a grocery sack off the counter as matching the movement in a bicep curl; the initial effort is the greatest. Machines, on the other hand, generally work with equal resistance throughout the lift, which does not match real-life movement mechanics. A free-weight workout, by duplicating the natural-lifting movement, results in a greater degree of "functional fitness," i.e., it better prepares you to lift or maneuver heavy objects outside the gym.

With the wide variety of equipment and benches available in a gym, a free-weight workout allows far greater variety than machines, and gives you a much wider range of exercise choices. For any given exercise, you can choose a flat bench, an incline bench, or a decline bench, and you can even vary the angle of the latter two. You can use any of the three benches for various exercises targeting different muscle groups or even different parts of the same muscle. Different grip positions are possible within a given exercise. There are a number of bars available, each designed to target the muscle from a different angle. When working out on machines, exercises are limited to the design of the machine.

Free weights are better at stimulating the muscle, and more muscle stimulus means faster results. You can be creative with free weights, as long as you are aware of proper body mechanics. Muscles are challenged by change and spontaneity. They respond more quickly to the variety of movement patterns available when training with barbells and dumbbells. On the other hand, weight machines limit the muscle involvement to one precise movement pattern.

Machines are valuable for certain special sections of the population, including older adults, handicapped and obese exercisers, and extremely weak people whose muscles are atrophied from being bedridden or because they are recovering from an injury.

Machines can also add variety to a workout. If you train in a facility where you have access to both free weights and weight machines, it won't hurt to use both. A machine workout can be used as a form of "active rest" on a rest day. Or you can interject weight-machine exercises into your routine to lessen the intensity of a

To make those biceps really work, do EZ Bar curls on a preacher bench. Doing front shoulder raises with a plate is an alternative to training with dumbbells.

training session. But don't make weight machines your equipment of choice. Free weights are what it's all about. As time goes on, and more and more people discover the many benefits of working out with free weights, the machine manufacturers will try harder and harder to match what barbells and dumbbells, and human ingenuity, have been capable of for years.

There are varied reasons why people train with weights, and not every one falls into a single category of another. Some train with specific exercises to enhance performance in a particular sport. Some train to increase bone mass, which helps prevent or even reverse osteoporosis, and some lift weights as part of a rehabilitation program.

Many people get into weight training just to improve their shape and tone, then find as a bonus that there are many other physical and psychological benefits to this form of exercise. In fact, people who *don't* do any resistance training are subjecting themselves to unnecessary health risks. In the first chapter of this book, we'll look at the many benefits of weight training, aside from sculpting your body. Read on—this information will increase your motivation to stick to your program!

Chapter 1

Why Exercise?

Weight Control

To shape your body the way you want it, you need to adopt a dual approach. First, you need to develop and tone your muscles through the exercises in this book. Second, and just as important, you need to maintain a healthy level of body fat, so that those sleek, toned muscles are visible to the outside world.

Perhaps the single most widespread reason that people exercise is to achieve and maintain a healthy body weight. But losing weight through exercise isn't simply a matter of burning-off calories while you are working out. Resistance training in particular helps you lose body fat in more subtle ways—more on this later.

First, let's look at the importance of aerobic exercise in body shaping. Aerobic activities, or sustained exercise that makes you sweat and keeps your heart pumping, help eliminate that extra body fat that can cover up even well-developed muscles.

The amount of fat you burn during aerobic exercise is dependent on your fitness level. A trained athlete burns fat sooner after exercise starts than someone who is moderately fit; a "couch potato" takes even longer to start burning fat, and even then burns it at a slower rate than a fit individual. Even during non-aerobic physical activities or at rest, a sedentary person burns fat at a much slower rate than someone who is active.

Having extra body fat slows down the metabolism, which makes it less efficient. Aerobic exercise temporarily raises the metabolism, so you have more energy and are also burning more calories.

Find an aerobic activity you like (otherwise you won't stick with it), then get up and do it 30 minutes to an hour most days of the week. You'll look better, feel better, be healthier, and have more energy!

Resistance Training and Metabolism

"Metabolism" refers to the body's chemical and physiological processes that provide energy—energy to do everything from thinking and breathing, to running a marathon.

Your metabolic rate is the speed at which your body burns calories. The higher your metabolic rate, the more efficiently you are getting energy to your cells, and the more calories you're burning. As we all know, burning more calories means you can eat more without gaining weight!

Metabolic rate is influenced by six factors. The good news is that most of them are under your control—that means you have the power to raise your metabolism, have more energy, and maintain a healthy and attractive body weight without depriving yourself of food! Let's look at the factors that determine your metabolic rate.

Body Composition The ratio of lean to fat tissue in your body is the biggest factor in determining your metabolic rate. This ratio is commonly referred to in terms of your "percent body fat." The lower your percent body fat, the higher your ratio of lean to fat tissue, and the higher your metabolic rate. Lean tissue includes bone, muscle, organs, blood, etc. We know all too well what fat is.

You can change your body composition by gaining lean muscle and bone mass, and by losing fat. Resistance training adds muscle and bone mass. Aerobic exercise and correct nutrition helps drop fat. The combination of resistance training, aerobic exercise, and proper eating dramatically affects body composition.

Reducing your percent body fat increases your metabolism because muscle tissue burns more calories just to maintain itself, even when at rest. Obese people have slow metabolisms and thus tend to get fatter and fatter because their bodies aren't burning calories efficiently. If you've got a healthy ratio of muscle to fat, your internal engine will be revving at a higher speed both when you're active and when you're not. The result? More energy for all the activities in your life, and less tendency to put on weight!

Activity Level Exercise temporarily boosts metabolic rate not just while you're exercising but for a while afterwards. The longer and harder you exercise, the greater the temporary boost. You can burn a lot of calories during the period of that temporary boost!

Also, remember that muscle is active tissue; fat is inactive. More muscle means your body is generating more energy. When people tone and develop their muscles, they find that they naturally tend to become more active and use their muscles more in everyday life. The beautiful thing about this is that as your activity level increases, you maintain and build your muscles and reduce your body fat. If you do resistance exercise to build muscle, and also maintain a generally active lifestyle, you create a positive feedback loop that reinforces your increased metabolic rate, energizes you, and makes it easier to become more fit and stay strong and healthy.

If, on the other hand, you opt for a sedentary lifestyle, the result will be a negative feedback loop: as your activity level is reduced, you'll have less muscle mass and your metabolic rate also decreases. As a result, you need fewer calories to maintain your body weight. Most people don't decrease their caloric intake to match their declining needs. If you don't cut down on calories, your weight goes up and percent body fat increases. Because fat is inactive tissue, that further slows down the metabolism, and you need still fewer calories. This self-reinforcing "vicious circle" makes overweight and sedentary people fatter and fatter. The way out is to convert from a sedentary to an active lifestyle, build muscle with resistance training, and get onto that positive feedback loop instead.

Use of a caliper device on several body areas provides an accurate measurement of body fat.

Diet What you eat, how much, and when are all important factors in determining your metabolic rate. In general, eating temporarily raises your metabolism. You've probably heard about the importance of breakfast—eating a healthy breakfast, containing complex carbohydrates and a low fat source of protein, will "kick start" your metabolism in the morning. But here's a more recent discovery that may go against what you've been told: eating small portions throughout the day keeps the metabolism revved up and can actually help you maintain a healthy body weight! Of course, this won't work if your snacks are cookies, potato chips, and ice cream. But "grazing" throughout the day on light, healthy foods is an excellent habit to get into. Try packing foods like baby carrots, pretzels, air-popped popcorn, bagels, apples and nonfat yogurt into your lunch—and you don't need to wait until lunch time to start eating them!

There are two eating habits to avoid if you want to raise your metabolism. First, you should know that hard-to-digest foods, most notably red meat, slow down the metabolism. Second, eating huge portions at one sitting clogs up the metabolic wheel and prevents it from turning very fast. Sumo wrestlers, who are trying to gain fat, do so by eating one huge meal every day for this reason.

Age As we get older our resting metabolism tends to slow down. However, this won't happen to you nearly as soon or as quickly if you're staying active and exercising regularly. The decrease in metabolic rate with age is primarily, if not entirely, due to the typical loss of muscle mass and the change in the fat-to-lean ratio. As we saw earlier, the less muscle mass you have, the fewer calories you burn even while resting.

To prevent loss of muscle mass as you age, you need to do some form of weight-bearing exercise. The most effective way by far is resistance training—lifting weights.

Hormones Thyroid hormone, in particular, helps regulate metabolic rate. Those with hypoactive or hyperactive thyroids suffer reduced or increased metabolic rates. If you suspect a thyroid problem, see your doctor. Medications are available which can compensate.

Genetics Genetic predisposition does play a role in determining your metabolic rate, but its effect is relatively minor. Since you can't change your genes anyway, focus on the factors above that you can influence!

As we've seen, strength training helps you achieve and maintain a healthy body weight in two ways: Not only are you burning calories directly through the exercise activity itself, but you're simultaneously increasing your body's calorie-burning rate by adding muscle and raising your metabolism. Muscle burns more energy (calories) because it is active tissue.

Weight lifting builds muscle faster and better than any other form of exercise. The overall effect on your metabolism can be dramatic: training with weights three times a week increases the calories a person burns by about 15%. If you don't increase your caloric intake, your body will burn that extra 15% from its stored calories, i.e., you'll burn off body fat! Every pound of muscle added to the body burns about 35 extra calories per day, or about 3 to 4 pounds of fat per year.

Without exercise, during each decade the typical adult loses about five pounds of lean body weight (muscle), gains approximately fifteen pounds of fat, and suffers a 5% drop in his or her resting metabolism. These numbers make it perfectly clear why everyone needs to exercise, and continue to do so throughout an entire lifetime.

Weight Training vs. Adult-Onset Diabetes

Adult-onset diabetes, or "diabetes type II," is a debilitating, often fatal disease that strikes about 1800 Americans every day—that's over 650,000 new cases a year! The majority of victims are over forty years old. Approximately nine out of ten cases of diabetes are type II. Ironically, most if not all of these cases are preventable.

Adult-onset diabetes affects the body's ability to use sugar. This disease disrupts normal energy metabolism both at rest and during physical activity.

As people grow older they tend to become less active, lose muscle, and gain body fat. This is especially true in modern American culture. Those who fail to maintain their muscle mass as they age, through an active lifestyle and/or resistance training, increase their risk of developing diabetes. To understand why, let's take a look at how the body manufactures and stores energy for its daily needs.

We make use of the sugars and starches that we consume by changing them into glucose. Glucose is carried in the bloodstream to the body's various tissues, but mostly to the muscles. For glucose to enter the muscle, insulin (a hormone made by the pancreas) must be present.

In a healthy person, any glucose that is not immediately needed for energy is stored in the muscles. If there is more glucose available than the muscles can accommodate, then the excess glucose finds its way to the liver, where it is converted to fat.

If you haven't got much muscle tissue, you lack glucose storage sites. The level of glucose in the bloodstream ("blood sugar") can become abnormally high. This forces the pancreas to work harder to produce more insulin, trying to get the glucose out of the bloodstream and into the muscle cells. Eventually the pancreas can wear out from overuse. The result is an impaired ability to manufacture insulin, or type II diabetes. The body's ability to use and store glucose is damaged. Diabetes, if left uncontrolled, can lead to heart disease, kidney failure, nerve dysfunction, stroke, high blood pressure, high cholesterol levels, and ulcers of the feet.

So what does weight training have to do with diabetes? Weight lifting builds muscle faster than any other form of exercise. Remember, if you've developed your muscles, then you have plenty of storage space for glucose. Your pancreas has less work to do, and you are less likely to develop diabetes. If you are already diabetic, weight training is an essential part of controlling the disease so that you can still live a normal life.

Weight-Bearing Exercise vs. Osteoporosis

Osteoporosis is the progressive weakening of the bones due to mineral loss. It causes bones to become less and less dense, creating a stooped posture and increasing the risk of broken bones. This latter risk especially must be taken seriously. For example, if you fail to protect your bone density, a simple fall in your golden years can break your hip, and few individuals over sixty-five or seventy ever completely recover from a broken hip. Very often, in fact, a broken hip starts a downward health spiral that leads to death within two or three

Key Lifestyle Factors Contributing to Osteoporosis

- Poor diet, including too much consumption of:
  alcohol—high consumption interferes with calcium absorption
  red meat—diets high in animal protein increase calcium excretion. Meat, in particular, is an acidic food. Calcium is excreted in high amounts to neutralize the acid
  sodium—too much salt causes the elimination of calcium through excretion
  soda—phosphates found in soda interfere with the absorption of calcium into the body.
- A diet that does not contain enough dark green vegetables, calcium foods (people over 50 need 1000–1800 mg. of calcium a day), vitamin D.
- Smoking—quit!
- Stress—we all have it, but we can learn to manage it effectively.
- A sedentary lifestyle—exercise!
- In women, being below 12 percent body fat for long periods of time. Being this thin can interfere with the menstrual cycle. Menstruation can even stop. This causes a drop in the production of estrogen, which in turn causes mineral loss from bones. If you are a woman and are not having your period, gain weight! If an eating disorder or psychological problem is at the root of it, get help—your long-term health is at serious risk!

years. Women are especially vulnerable to osteoporosis, but men can be affected too.

Doing some form of weight-bearing exercise regularly is crucial to the prevention of osteoporosis. Calcium is deposited in the bones in proportion to the amount of stress (load) placed on them. Bones adapt to such exercise by becoming denser and stronger, so they can provide sufficient support for the muscles. Lifting weights is the fastest, most effective way to preserve and increase bone mass (other than using prescription drugs), because it is also the fastest, most effective way to build muscle.

For weight lifting to affect bone density, you must lift enough weight to overload the muscle—you have to train to the point of "muscle failure." We'll show you how in this book. But for now, please note that training to muscle failure does not mean you need to spend a lot of time in the gym. It is a matter of technique, not time. If you begin even a modest program of resistance training and stick with it for the rest of your life, you're helping to guarantee that you'll maintain your health and vitality to a ripe old age.

For your bones to get the maximum benefit possible from weight training, it is a good idea to become aware of some other things you can do to decrease your risk of osteoporosis. Examine the chart on the page opposite and make a decision to choose now to eliminate or at least reduce your personal risk.

The osteoporosis risk factors listed for you in the chart opposite are all things that you have control over. It is also useful to be aware of the uncontrollable risk factors in the development of osteoporosis. If you fit into any of the following categories, there's all the more reason to do everything you can to minimize your controllable risks, especially through weight training!

- Fair skinned
- Small boned—have less bone mass to begin with naturally
- Thin—bones are not normally as strong because they are not required to support a higher body weight. (This is *not* a good reason to put on weight, just make up for it through weight training!)
- Family history of osteoporosis
- Age, especially women who have passed through menopause. Estrogen helps prevent bone mineral loss, and after menopause estrogen production nearly ceases.

A long-term commitment to weight training is the single best decision you can make to prevent osteoporosis.

Exercise and Heart Disease

Heart Disease Risk Factors There are a number of "risk factors" for coronary artery disease (heart disease). Some of them you have control over; a few you don't. The controllable risk factors are:

1. High cholesterol, which can be managed by eating a low-cholesterol diet, exercising regularly, and taking medication if necessary. Weight training and aerobic exercise help you lose body fat and thus reduce cholesterol. In addition, regular aerobic exercise increases your HDLs (the "good cholesterol"). HDLs sweep the LDLs ("bad cholesterol") out of your bloodstream, thus lowering your risk of heart disease.

2. High blood pressure can also be managed by diet, aerobic exercise, stress reduction, and medication if necessary. Because aerobic exercise lowers your overall blood pressure, it helps reduce your risk of stroke as well as heart disease.

3. Cigarette smoking, which can be managed only by quitting.

4. Lack of exercise, for which the cure is, of course, to exercise regularly.

5. Obesity, which is managed by diet, counseling, and exercise! Both aerobic exercise and weight training help you lose body fat. That in turn reduces your risk not only of heart disease, but also of stroke, adult-onset diabetes, and some cancers.

The heart disease risk factors that you can't control are fewer:

1. Family history or an inherited predisposition for heart disease.

2. Age—Menopausal women are at greater risk after their bodies stop producing estrogen. Estrogen replacement therapy can reduce this risk, but long-term use of estrogen can increase other health risks. The best solution is to change bad lifestyle habits.
3. Gender—Males are automatically at higher risk.

Don't be at all discouraged just because you fall into some of the above groups. Even if you're an older adult, from a family with a history of heart disease, your chances of avoiding heart disease are good as long as you eat a very low-fat, mostly vegetarian diet, do regular aerobic exercise, don't smoke, maintain a healthy weight, and manage your stress.

On the other hand, even if you're young, female, and not aware of any family history, you're not immune. Protect yourself by avoiding the controllable risk factors as well.

Cardiovascular exercise is an important part of an overall body-shaping program.

You may have noticed that exercise shows up as a solution to four out of the five controllable risk factors. You can see how important exercise is in preventing heart disease! A sedentary lifestyle is a major risk factor for developing cardiovascular disease. Doing regular exercise, especially aerobic exercise, is one of the most important steps you can take to reduce your risk of heart disease. So, in addition to your weight-training regimen, find an aerobic activity you like and do it for at least twenty (preferably thirty) minutes, most days of the week. Some different types of aerobic exercise are brisk walking (walk as if you have some place to be and are running late), jogging, running, cycling, step aerobics, and aerobic exercise classes.

The heart is a muscle. For it to remain strong and healthy it needs to be worked, just like the other muscles in our body. Aerobic exercise strengthens the heart. It takes time for your heart to actually become stronger, but its functions (oxygen delivery out to the rest of your body) improve almost immediately. When your heart becomes stronger, more oxygen can be circulated to your body with less work (fewer heartbeats). Eventually your heart rate (heartbeats per minute) lowers because your heart has become more efficient at supplying your body with the oxygen it needs to live. A slower heart rate (fewer beats per minute) means your heart may last longer because it doesn't have to work so hard.

Weight training, as important as it is, doesn't have the heart-strengthening benefit of aerobic exercise. That is why weight training must be part of a comprehensive fitness program. There are in fact three major cornerstones of physical fitness: aerobic exercise, resistance training, and flexibility work (stretching). If you do all three, not only are you on track to live a long, disease-free life, but you're also helping ensure that you'll feel as good as possible while you're at it.

Exercise and Arthritis

Resistance exercise eases the pain of osteoarthritis and rheumatoid arthritis.

Lifting weights strengthens the muscles and joints. When exercises are performed correctly, range of motion in the joints increases. Full range of motion means the joints are more flexible. Weight training also decreases the risk of injuries which aggravate the afflicted joints, because stronger muscles make better shock absorbers and better joint stabilizers.

People with arthritis are often obese, partly because arthritis makes them so inactive. Obesity aggravates the effects of arthritis. An exercise program that includes strength training and walking can improve arthritis symptoms by helping the sufferer lose weight.

If you have arthritis, check with your doctor before starting any exercise program.

Stress Management

When we are under stress, our bodies release certain hormones and chemicals which increase our heart rate, metabolism, blood pressure, respiratory rate, and muscle tension. This heightened state is often referred to as the "fight or flight" syndrome. In most stressful situations we cannot fight or flee, so our bodies don't have an appropriate way to handle these conditions.

Unfortunately, the chemicals created by our bodies under stress have a negative impact on our immune systems. Too much stress is not good for our health.

If you are under continuous stress, whatever the source, your body's reaction can result in any number of physical and/or emotional symptoms. Headaches, stomachaches, ulcers, digestive problems, and insomnia are a few examples of physical problems related to excessive stress. If you don't have a way to reduce your stress, and it becomes chronic, there is evidence it can lead to or worsen coronary artery disease, high blood pressure, and the risk of stroke.

Some emotional problems brought on by stress include edginess, aggression, a decline in libido, depression, anxiety attacks, loss of a sense of well-being, feelings of ill will, boredom, and a reluctance to get up and face the day.

How can you avoid these dangers? First, if something is a continual source of stress in your life, try to resolve or eliminate it. If that isn't possible, learn to accept it. Second, increase your stress threshold—your ability to take stressful situations in stride. The best way to become more stress-resistant is to take good care of your health. Most important, get regular exercise. Also, eat a healthy diet, don't drink or smoke, and cut back on caffeine. Devote some time each week to some form of genuine relaxation. Develop close relationships with friends and family. The more people you know and care about, the greater your resources for emotional support. Make long-term commitments to someone and something. Long-term goals often make short-term problems easier to handle.

Strengthening the Immune System

The human immune system appears to function better when one exercises regularly. According to recent studies, physically fit people get fewer colds and upper-respiratory tract infections. This is probably because even moderate exercise increases the circulation of your natural "killer" cells in your bloodstream, such as T-cells and immunoglobulin. These cells protect our bodies from foreign invaders. The increase lasts only a few hours, but apparently that's long enough to ward off some infections. But don't overdo it; too much exercise is probably worse than not enough.

Bone and Muscle Strength for Balance and Posture

After the age of 25, we lose from a quarter to a half pound of muscle each year in the absence of exercise. This loss of muscle, and the corresponding loss of bone mass, has a terrible impact on the quality of life for older people.

Their posture stoops, their bones become brittle, they become weak, they lose their balance, and they are easily injured.

Strength training is the most effective way to prevent this degenerative process from occurring. By lifting weights, it's possible to actually reverse the shrinkage and build more muscle and bone mass.

Strong muscles help maintain good posture, they enhance the ability to balance, and they help prevent injuries. As you lift weights, you not only strengthen the muscles and build bone mass, you also strengthen the connective tissue (tendons and ligaments) within the working joints. Strong connective tissue and denser muscles make better shock absorbers. They stabilize the joints. They hold the body erect and keep it in proper alignment. In all these ways, they lessen the potential for injury.

More muscle strength is helpful for all physical activities. The stronger you are, the more successful you are at sport performance, and everyday activities become easier.

Muscle atrophy (shrinkage) often contributes to pain in the body. For instance, weak muscles in the lower back and abdominals are a key factor in low back pain. Another example is neck pain. If you sit at a desk all day, neck strength can decrease up to 30% between 9:00 and 5:00. This can lead to neck pain. If the muscles and connective tissue in and around the neck are strong, this strength decrease may have less impact, which translates to less, if any, pain. Also, strong muscles may lessen the pain caused by chronic problems, such as arthritis.

It's harder to be independent and self-reliant if you don't have the strength to support those attitudes. Both the act of working out and the results you get from the process provide positive reinforcement and can help improve your self-image and self-concept.

Think ahead—when you're in your 80s you'll want to look up and out at the world, not down at the ground. Start weight training now, so that all your years can be experienced fully.

More Energy!

Too many people make the excuse that they are too tired to exercise or they need to save their energy. What these people don't realize is that exercise actually energizes the body and reduces fatigue—those who exercise regularly have more energy for the rest of their activities than those who do not! There are several reasons for this paradoxical effect. For starters, exercise increases your body's ability to utilize oxygen, which improves stamina, creates more vigor, and enhances your concentration. Also, regular exercise helps reduce muscle tension, a major cause of tiredness. And, on the cellular level, exercise encourages your body to manufacture more mitochondria, which is the place in the cell where energy is produced.

Exercise helps reduce your psychological response to stress, and unmanaged stress is probably the number one cause of fatigue in America today. Also, the extra energy generated by exercise can help you accomplish more and deal with the everyday pressures of life, which means you'll avoid some of the things that have tended to cause you stress.

Exercise helps you to relax, and regular exercise helps you to sleep better. A good night's sleep is always great for increasing energy levels.

Exercise improves self-image and gives you a feeling of accomplishment. These psychological factors have a huge impact on your energy levels. When you feel good about yourself you're more likely to want to go out into the world and explore life's possibilities.

Exercise invigorates your body both short term and long term. The biggest short-term gain is right after a bout of aerobic exercise. Your metabolism is higher than before you exercised and you're burning calories at an accelerated rate. The longer and harder you exercise, the greater the temporary metabolic boost.

Over the long term, exercise has a cumulative energy-boosting effect. Regular weight lifting builds muscle, and regular aerobic exercise burns fat. The combination of these

Meeting friends regularly "at the gym" to work out can spur you to stick to your training program.

two effects raises your metabolic rate—the rate at which your body burns calories while active or even at rest. A higher metabolic rate means that more energy is made available to your muscles all the time.

Lifting weights also boosts energy by improving glycogen storage—the means by which your body makes sugar available for energy. The carbohydrates in your food are broken down into glucose molecules, and stored in the muscles as glycogen. Think of your muscles as the gas tank in your car. With a bigger gas tank, you can store more fuel; thus your car will run for a longer period of time.

Similarly, the more muscle you have, the more space you have to store glycogen and the longer your body will run. You'll have more energy to get you through the day, without experiencing an afternoon slump. In fact, glucose metabolism can improve as much as 23% after just four months of regular strength training. On the other hand, if you don't have much muscle available for glycogen storage, not only will you have less energy available, but you'll also have a greater tendency to put on fat. Your body will circulate the excess glucose back to your liver, where it is converted into fat and then stored in your body's fat cells.

Exercise and Brain Function

Regular exercise increases the amount of oxygen delivered to the brain and improves mental agility. Your brain makes up only 2% of your body weight, but uses a full 25% of the glucose and oxygen you take in! Exercise increases your body's ability to take in and utilize oxygen. When you exercise, you saturate your body with oxygen; hence more oxygen becomes available for brain power. If you don't exercise, then as you get older your heart gets sluggish. Your arteries start to clog up. Blood flow to the tiny capillaries that nourish the brain cells can slow to a mere trickle. If you want to remain mentally alert and agile as you age, do some kind of exercise most days of the week.

Exercise also activates the sections of your brain that control movement and balance. A long-term exercise regime, including resistance training, can keep your motor skills strong into old age, allow you to stay coordinated, and help maintain your balance.

Chapter 2

Starting Out Right

Injury Prevention

If you follow some basic rules, you can look forward to a lifetime of resistance training. The single most important way to prevent injury is simply to use good form while exercising. The exercise descriptions in this book will tell you how to do that. Pay special attention to the "Notes" at the end of each exercise description, and re-read them from time to time until correct form has become a habit.

Like good form, good workout habits are essential to avoiding injury. This means, first off, never skip your warm-up. Also, get plenty of sleep, eat healthy food, and drink plenty of water. Read, re-read, and apply safety rules, and get a weight belt if lifting heavy weights.

Weight Belts

When doing certain exercises, you may want to wear a weight belt (shown below). Weight belts are useful when training the chest, back, and shoulders, and for leg exercises done in a standing position. Unless you have lower-back trouble, a weight belt is only necessary when lifting heavier weights.

Weight belts come in a variety of materials. Find one that feels good on your body and fills your needs. For more about weight belts, and other accessories, see Chapter 9.

Dumbbell-Handling Techniques

When you work out with dumbbells, there is a specific way to lift the weights off the floor and into the starting position, and a specific way of putting them back down again.

Most dumbbell exercises are done on a bench. Before you begin, have the dumbbells on the floor beside the bench. Pick one dumbbell up at a time and place it on the top of your leg, then do the same with the other. Next, kick one leg up, so you're simultaneously pushing with the thigh and lifting with your hand. In this way, bring the dumbbell up to shoulder level. Then do the same with the other dumbbell. Next, if the exercise calls for it, lower your back onto the bench.

When you're finished with your set, bring the dumbbells back to your shoulders; then, one at a time, put them back on top of each leg. Next, pull yourself up into a sitting position (the weight of the dumbbells helps you do this). From the sitting position, place each dumbbell, one at a time, back onto the floor.

This will all seem unnecessary, unless you are working with heavier weights. Still, it's best to use this proper method, even if the dumbbells you are using now aren't that heavy. You won't have to relearn technique when you graduate to heavier workloads.

Body Mechanics and Exercise Performance

The most important factors for a safe exercise routine are holding your body properly and performing the exercise movements correctly. Exercises done with these things in mind also deliver the best results. Never compromise safety for the sake of a quicker workout, an easier workout, or any other reason.

While performing any weight-lifting exercise, keep in mind these basic safety rules. Read and re-read them frequently. Remember, safety first, and safe form equals effective form.

Safety Rules

- Never lock your joints when exercising. Hyperextension (locked joints) places heavy stress on the joint without further benefit to the working muscle.
- Never arch your back. Sometimes arching the back makes an exercise seem easier, but in reality, you're putting your back at high risk for injury.
- Always work with a neutral spine. Never tilt your head up and back or forward and down. Both positions compromise the small cervical (neck) vertebrae and put them at risk for injury.
- Avoid hyperflexing (over-stretching) your joints. Repeated hyperflexing of the connective tissue in the joints may lead to joint laxity (loose joints).
- When doing an exercise from a standing position, place your feet wide enough apart so you feel stable and balanced.
- Keep the weights close to your body. To avoid buildup of momentum, make sure not to swing the weights.
- Keep the abdominal and buttocks muscles tight and tucked. This will help to stabilize the trunk of your body and protect the lower back.
- When doing exercises from a seated position, keep your feet flat on the floor, knees forming a right angle. This will help stabilize the lower back.
- Concentrate, and strive for a controlled movement in both phases of the lift (lifting and lowering the weight). The exercise will not only be safer, but harder to do, therefore more beneficial.
- Always warm up before training.
- Drink plenty of water while training. Drink before you feel the need; never allow your body to become thirsty.
- Wear comfortable, unrestrictive clothing.
- Breathe correctly. Exhale on exertion, and inhale while lowering the weight back down. This is a hard-and-fast rule; there are no exceptions. The reason is that if you hold your breath while exerting (lifting the weight), the thoracic pressure in and around your chest muscles can increase to the point where you cut down on the amount of blood returning to your heart. This can cause dizziness, a blackout, or even a ruptured blood vessel.
- Rest between sets long enough so that you are able to complete the next set without stopping. Larger muscle groups need more rest time. If, for example, you are doing heavy squats (which work the large muscles in the buttocks and legs), you will need a longer recovery time between sets than if you are doing bicep curls (which primarily work one muscle in the arm). Beginners also need more rest time.
- When working your legs, walk around between sets instead of sitting down. This way the blood will keep circulating and not pool in the lower extremities.
- Give your body a rest of 48 hours before training the same muscle group again. This allows time for tissue recovery.
- Take some time off now and then, and don't overtrain.
- Keep a positive attitude, focus on the small changes, and affirm that you are reaching your goals.

Working Through "Sticking Points"

Anyone who lifts weights is bound to run into a "sticking point" occasionally in certain exercises—a part of the lift that you can't move through without "cheating." About 99% of weight lifters take the easy way out and cheat on their form. But there is a better way.

The usual way individuals respond to a sticking point is by sacrificing good form. They either use momentum and swing the weight through the range of motion, or they contort their body in a way that the weight can be jerked through the sticking point. Both methods can lead to injury, and neither of them make you stronger. Swinging, jerking, and contorting simply do not lead to functional strength—they lead to more swinging, jerking, and contorting...and to injury.

The real solution to training through a sticking point is simple. Reduce the resistance and practice moving through the limited range of motion at the point where the sticking occurs. For real strength gains to be made, the weaker part of the muscle (think of it as the weakest link in a chain) must be the target of controlled partial rep work (see page 138).

No one likes to reduce the amount of weight he or she is lifting. But in this case, it works. As soon as the weaker part of the muscle gets stronger, you can return to full range of motion training without having to cheat.

Joint Conditioning

Weight training not only strengthens the muscles and bones, but also the connective tissue in the joints. The connective tissues most affected by weight lifting are tendons, which hold muscle to bone. The stronger the tendons, the stronger the joints. Strong joints increase joint stability, which plays an important role in injury prevention, both in and out of the gym.

As a general practice, lift the weights through the joint's full range of motion as instructed in each exercise. When you become more advanced, this training principle may be modified with partial rep work. But partial range of motion exercises are prescribed only after the muscles and joints are fully conditioned and are capable of handling the kind of stress created by that type of training.

Even after your muscles and joints are conditioned, avoid the temptation to lift too heavy a weight. You must always consider not only your muscular strength (how much resistance the muscles can handle) but also your joint strength (how much resistance the connective tissue can handle). Good form is compromised when you try to lift more than what your body can handle. Poor form usually leads to injury or to, at the least, a less potent workout. Poor form is the biggest enemy to building bigger, shapelier, stronger muscles safely.

Besides increasing your likelihood of injury, training with poor form develops "artificial strength," where you think you're developing strength in one particular muscle group, while in reality you're depending on other muscle groups to assist with an exercise. That cuts into your true strength gains.

Rest—An Elemental Need

Working out with weights creates microscopic muscle contusions (ruptures) and causes muscle spasms. Lactic acid also builds up. These processes are part of muscle development; they are signs that you stimulated the muscle and had a good workout.

When you rest, events occur at the cellular level that cause the muscle and joint structures to change. Without the needed rest, these cellular changes don't have a chance to take place. The result may be injury, or at the very least a reduction in strength gains.

It's not necessary to understand all of these physical processes, but it may be helpful to understand a few. It's during the resting phase that contractile proteins within the muscle increase in size and number. That increase is what makes the muscle bigger, harder, and stronger. Tendons, the connective tissues associated with muscle, become thicker and stronger, making the joint more stable and durable. The number of capillaries within the muscle increase in order to handle the increased amount of oxygen flowing to the muscle. Bones become denser and stronger in order to handle the new stress placed on them by the muscle.

A 48-hour resting phase is as necessary to muscle development as the training itself. All the programs in this book are designed to give the prime movers (primary working muscles) a 48-hour rest before training them again. That doesn't mean you can't work out every day if you want to. It does mean that if you expect to make real progress, you must not train the same muscle or muscle group within a 48-hour period.

Overtraining

How much exercise is too much? If exercise is causing you pain and you're ignoring your body's need for rest, then you're overdoing it. You may be psychologically addicted to exercise, or "exercise dependent," to the point of unhealthiness. An early indication of exercise dependency is how someone deals with an injury. Someone who is exercise dependent tries to work through the injury instead of taking the necessary time off to let it heal.

Exercise shouldn't be the focus of your life. If your workouts interfere with family, work, or life's everyday obligations, you are spending too much time at the gym.

Often, overexercisers feel edgy or even depressed if they miss a training session. Many are obsessed with staying thin, often maintaining a body weight that is too low for optimum health. Overexercisers exercise to have a "perfect body" instead of better health, and they often lie about how much they exercise.

Some symptoms of overtraining include:

- Elevated resting pulse rate
- Loss of appetite
- Recurring colds, illness, or rashes
- Insomnia
- Lethargy in other activities besides working out
- Frequent nightmares
- Feeling tired or drained
- Recurring injuries
- Continued soreness in the same muscle

If you have an elevated resting pulse rate, and two or more of the other symptoms, you're probably overtraining. If your resting pulse rate is normal, then your problems are probably not due to overtraining; look instead for psychological factors in your life that could be causing the symptoms.

People who are addicted to exercise usually won't acknowledge it, not even to themselves. Such denial is typical of all forms of compulsive behavior. But there is a point where even the compulsive exerciser becomes injured or exhausted and has to take some time off. If this time off leads to behavioral changes such as moodiness, irritability, or depression, it's time to do some self-examination. Exercise should be seen as a way to become and stay healthy, not an obsession for its own sake.

So how much exercise is enough? Optimally, everyone should take one day a week off from all forms of vigorous exercise. At the least, take a day off every week from resistance training and a different day off from aerobic exercise. This is necessary in order for your muscles, connective tissue, and joints to recover. If you work out with weights every day, you're setting yourself up for joint injury and muscle depletion. That's true even if you don't train the same muscle group two days in a row, because those muscles will still be taxed as assisting or stabilizing muscles and won't ever get the full rest that they occasionally need.

When physically conditioned, you can safely exercise aerobically twenty minutes to an hour six days of the week, and you can lift weights safely up to five or six times per week. Also, each major muscle group in your body except the abdominals needs a 48-hour rest before you train that muscle group again. This allows time for the physiological adaptations to take place within the muscle. If you train the same muscle group every day, you'll certainly create negative results.

From time to time, it's also important to take more than a day off from lifting weights, preferably a few days. We're not suggesting that you become a couch potato during these periods. Instead, try "active rest" or cross training—engage in alternate forms of exercise. For instance, swim laps in place of lifting weights, go for a brisk walk or a jog instead of training your legs in the gym. The idea is to make a change in your training program that gives the body a chance to recover before beginning another rigorous training cycle. Participate in activities that challenge the body and mind in creative and different ways.

Recognizing and Managing Injuries

There are four kinds of soreness or pain that can result from lifting weights. The first two below are signs that you're doing it right; the other two mean that you've injured yourself.

"The Burn" Lactic acid builds up in your muscles as you work them. The lactic acid is what prevents you from doing more reps. It also causes a slight burning sensation in the muscle; thus the expression "No pain, no gain!" As soon as you finish your set and bring oxygen to the muscle, the lactic acid is dispersed and the sensation disappears.

Localized Soreness It is normal for your muscles to feel sore for 48 to 72 hours after a hard workout. Good ways to relieve soreness are slow stretching, warm compresses, a hot bath, rest, or massage. If the soreness persists for more than three days, you may have strained a muscle.

Strains A strain (or "pulled muscle") usually appears suddenly. It results when the muscle or tendon is over-stretched, resulting in tiny tears. If you follow our safety rules and avoid overtraining, strains should not occur.

Should you strain a muscle, first and foremost, stop your workout. You'll need at least a few days' rest—more if the strain is severe. When you do start lifting weights again, start out considerably lighter than usual, until you're sure you have completely recovered. The formula for treating strains is RICE—rest, ice, compression, and elevation. Of these, rest and ice are the most important. Aspirin also helps ease pain and reduce swelling. If the strain persists or seems serious, better see your doctor.

Muscle strains heal well with proper attention and rest. But if you don't treat a strain or give yourself time to recover, the injury can become chronic.

Sprains A sprain is a severe injury and is very rare in weight training. It occurs when the ligament is pulled or twisted beyond its maximum range of motion, most often happening in the ankles. A sprain always happens suddenly, and is accompanied by severe bruising and swelling. If you suspect you have a sprain, see your doctor. In the meantime, use the RICE treatment mentioned under strains.

Don't be scared off by the above cautions. Weight training is one of the safest forms of exercise, if performed correctly—as laid out in this book.

The Proper Warm-Up

Why warm up? There are important physiological reasons why warming up prevents injury and increases the benefits of your workout—we'll cover those in just a minute. But equally important, warming up prepares us psychologically for a workout. We go into the gym, or wherever it is we train, with a mood and mind set created by whatever has happened to us so far that day. We might be frustrated because we were stuck in traffic, we may be feeling angry or sad, we could be anxious because of job stresses or worried about an important exam we're about to take. A warm-up helps put us in the present. We become body conscious, and a body–mind connection is made that will result in a more effective as well as a more enjoyable workout.

Physiologically speaking, a warm-up elevates the core temperature and individual muscles of your body, which makes exercise safer. Cold, stiff muscles and joints are at higher risk of injury than those that have been properly warmed up.

A warm-up also increases respiration and heart rate and stroke volume. How fast you breathe, how fast the heart beats, and the amount of blood passing through the heart muscle each time it beats are all measures of how much blood is circulating out to your body. The red blood cells (hemoglobin) in the bloodstream are what carry the oxygen to your muscles. So warming up allows more oxygen to be delivered more efficiently to the working muscles.

Without this rich supply of oxygen, your muscles won't work very effectively. One reason is that lactic acid, a by-product of muscle activity, builds up and prevents any further work. Oxygen disperses lactic acid and allows exercise to continue. Energy enzymes cannot function at full capacity in the presence of lactic acid. A good warm-up, and the oxygen it delivers to your muscles, increases the effectiveness of these enzymes by dispersing lactic acid. By warming up, you are more energized.

Another good reason to warm-up is that a warm, oxygenated muscle has greater flexibility. Flexibility helps prevent injuries.

Finally, warming up before a workout improves the viscosity of the synovial fluids that surround moveable joints. Think of the Tin Man in "The Wizard of Oz." He could move just fine once his joints were oiled. It's similar with people. A warm-up lubricates our joints, which allow us to move freely. Full, easy range of motion in all our moveable joints is a key factor in preventing joint injury.

How much of a warm-up should you do? Five to ten minutes on a stationary bike, treadmill, or StairMaster is enough. Do your warm-up exercise at an intensity that makes you break into a sweat. The more power necessary for a sport or activity, the more important the warm-up.

A warm-up is sometimes based on the dynamic movement of a specific sport or activity. Specific warm-ups use movements that are similar to the movements of the athlete's sport. In the case of weight lifting, a warm-up can consist in part of a weight lifting exercise that works the same muscles you will be training that day. Go ahead and start your prescribed exercise, but use a very light weight and do 10–15 reps. After this initial warm-up set, you'll be ready to start your routine using heavier resistance.

If you lift weights with cold, tight muscles, you're inviting injury. There won't be enough oxygen in the muscles to enable them to perform, and your energy enzymes will be slogging around in an acid bath. Both will cause early muscle fatigue. Early muscle fatigue leads to poor body mechanics and to possible joint and muscle injury.

The bottom line: without a warm-up your workouts will be less potent, more dangerous and not nearly as much fun.

Cooling Down

After aerobic exercise, cooling down might mean just going more slowly—switching from a run to a walk to slow down your heart rate. After a weight workout, the best way to cool down is to stretch all the muscles you trained in that session.

Breathe slowly and deeply while cooling down. To ensure the deepest relaxation, be aware of your body releasing the muscle's tension. Now would be a good time to do a visualization or to repeat to yourself one of your affirmations.

A cool-down period has both physical and psychological benefits. Psychologically, it reduces stress. A cool-down allows time for the body and the mind to relax. Slowing down the body automatically slows down the mind.

Physiologically, a cool-down does a number of important things. Cool-down stretching increases flexibility and helps retain full range of motion in the joints, which decreases the risk of joint injury. Cool-down stretching improves muscular balance and postural awareness. In general, a cool-down helps reduce muscle soreness by increasing the blood supply and nutrients going to the muscles and joints.

All workouts need a cool-down, but the higher the intensity level of a workout, the more important the cool-down becomes.

Make Workout Time Count

When you go to work out, in the gym or at home, you don't want to waste your time. Each workout should make a difference. Not a big difference, but a difference, nonetheless. The benefits of lifting weights are cumulative. Every workout does a little something to the muscle and bone. If you want your muscles to grow bigger, denser, and stronger, you have to train them harder than what they're used to.

To spark the physiological process that changes the muscle, you have to overload the muscle. If the muscle doesn't reach fatigue each time you train, then the workout is not hard enough. Of course, "hard" is a relative word. For a beginner, light weights and short training sessions can still equal a hard workout.

The overload principle is even more important when it comes to increasing bone mass. Bone mineral density will not increase unless there's a great deal of stress placed on the bones. Bones adapt to stress by becoming denser and stronger.

So make each workout matter. Even if you spend just 20 minutes training, make those 20 minutes as potent as possible. A good, hard workout—one where you train your muscles to failure or nearly to failure—will invigorate and empower you and give you more energy and self-confidence.

If you do something every day of your life (besides eating and sleeping), eventually you'll tend to get bored with the activity and lose interest in it. This is a common occurrence with exercise. When people first start to exercise they love the way it makes them feel—to the point where some people overdo it and forsake life's other activities. Eventually, because they can't keep up the pace they've set for themselves, they quit. Training is like anything in life—too much of a good thing and it no longer interests us. With exercise, there is also the potential for developing overuse injuries.

We recommend taking one day off from all planned exercise, every week. This short amount of total rest will not have any negative effect on your fitness level; on the contrary, time off from a heavy training schedule actually improves fitness. Also, a few times a year, take a week or two and go on a program of "active rest." "Active rest" means changing your exercise routine for a while and allowing your body a chance to recover before beginning another training cycle.

Active rest is a healthy alternative to total rest or inactivity. It can involve lowering the training frequency (work out fewer times per week), reducing the intensity of the training regimen (make the workouts easier), shortening the duration of an activity (train for a shorter period of time), or all of the above.

Active rest also can include cross-training, where you continue to exercise but do different activities. For example if you generally run and lift weights for fitness, "rest" by doing some swimming and cycling in their place.

Whatever you choose to do, the idea is to cut back on the daily demands of intense exercise to prevent overtraining. Give yourself some "active rest," and the result will be an increase in both your fitness and your enjoyment of your exercise program. You'll also be less susceptible to the injuries that often result from overtraining.

If you become compulsive about exercise, your commitment to it may not last very long. Let exercise and its many benefits enhance your life, not rule it.

Listen to your body. There are going to be days when you are scheduled to train and you don't feel up to it. Listen, and make sure you are not just looking for an excuse to be lazy.

Allow yourself to progress slowly in your workouts. Push yourself, but not to the point where you risk injuries. And be sensible! The long-term benefits are well worth it. A good motto to follow: "Train for Life."

Working Out at Home

Working out at home is convenient and can save you lots of time, but it presents its own special challenges. When you work out at a gym it's easier to focus on the task at hand,

because you don't have the distractions that often occur at home. There is no phone to answer, no favorite TV program competing for your attention, no children wanting you to play. Because your home is a more relaxed environment, it will probably be more difficult for you to concentrate on your workout. Here are some suggestions to make it easier:

Choose a time when there are as few distractions as possible. Hopefully this time coincides with a time when your energy level is high. If you really feel like a vigorous workout, it's of course easier to follow through and do it.

Be flexible, but try to train at the same time each day. Our bodies long for and respond well to routine. If possible, have a designated area for your workout, a place where you can leave your equipment. It's a lot easier not to have to haul everything out each time (bench, weights, gloves, belt, etc.), and then have to put it away again. Make sure your workout area is bright and airy with good air circulation. A mirror is helpful. It provides instant feedback on body form and function. Music is great, and unlike a gym you get to play what you like. Music motivates people. Virtually all gyms play upbeat music to inspire their patrons to "move." The same philosophy works at home.

Chapter 3

Nutrition

A Correctly Balanced Diet

To create the body shape you want, you need to adopt eating habits that will help you keep the fat off. Most people who succeed in adopting a healthy, low-fat diet find their motivation in the desire for a better appearance. But there's a far better reason—your health and longevity! The diet that best protects you against heart disease, against adult-onset diabetes, and against colon, prostate, ovarian, and breast cancer is a low-fat one—a largely vegetarian diet low in saturated fat (less than 7% of daily calories), and cholesterol (200 mg or less per day), with low levels of sodium (1800 mg or less per day), and plenty of foods rich in fiber.

The four basic food groups are a thing of the past. New research in nutrition shows that certain foods deserve much more emphasis than others in a healthy diet. A correctly balanced diet emphasizes complex carbohydrates (vegetables, fruits, rice, potatoes, yams, and grains—preferably whole grains). Next in emphasis come the protein foods (minus red meat). These are beans and legumes, white meat poultry without the skin, fish, and egg whites. Then low-fat dairy products, such as skim milk, low-fat or non-fat yogurt, and low-fat cottage cheese. Finally, in the smallest category of a healthy diet, are the things you should eat sparingly or not at all, including butter, oils, sweets and pastries, alcohol, red meat, and cheese. Red meat, cheese, and the skin of poultry are so high in fat and cholesterol that they do not belong with healthy low-fat protein sources.

Whether you're primarily concerned with your appearance, your health, or both, the most important single dietary guideline is to watch your fat consumption! Only 20% to 25% of your total daily calories should come from fat. Let's say you eat 1500 calories a day. 1500 times .25 equals 375, so you will be able to eat 375 calories a day from fat. There are 9 calories (to make the math easier, round up to 10) in one gram of fat, so divide 375 by 10 and you get 37.5 grams. So to eat 25% calories from fat at 1500 calories, you are allowed 37½ grams of fat each day.

A more general range is from 300 to 500 calories a day from fat. If you're in the high end one day, cut back on the fat calories the next. Remember, your ultimate goal is a well-balanced diet which provides all the essential nutrients for optimum health.

Some people find it easier to control their fat intake with reference to individual foods. The new food labels require packagers of most prepared foods to state the total number of calories and the calories from fat. As long as you avoid food products that get more than 25% of their calories from fat, you'll be meeting the overall goal.

Cutting back on dietary fat can be tricky; different methods work for different people. Going "cold turkey"—eliminating fatty foods and restricting your total diet to no more than 25% calories from fat—works best for many people. Others will find it easier to slowly reduce the frequency and amount of fatty foods. This tactic often ensures that fatty foods don't take on a forbidden status, which can make them harder to resist. Substituting non-fat varieties in place of their high-fat counterparts (e.g., non-fat frozen yogurt or sorbet in place of ice cream) is another strategy that works well. However you choose to do it, don't put it off. More and more evidence is coming in showing just how bad a high-fat diet is for your health, your heart, and your chances of living to a ripe old age.

Here is a list of some high-fat foods you should eliminate from your diet now. If you stop eating these foods, you will be cutting out the top ten sources of fat in the American diet.

- Whole and 2% lower-fat milk (skim or 1% is better)
- Margarine and butter
- Shortening
- Mayonnaise (some non-fat varieties are tasty substitutes)
- Salad dressing (oil-free brands are good)
- Cheese (soy cheese alternatives still tend to be high in fat)
- Ground beef, even the leanest
- Egg yolks (the whites are fine, but eat no more than two yolks a week)
- Ice cream (plenty of non-fat alternatives are now on the market)
- Peanut butter

A low-fat diet is so important in reaching your fitness goals (as well as for your health!) that we'll give you some more tips on the subject in a separate section toward the end of this chapter. First, let's look at your other basic dietary requirements.

Protein—How Much Is Enough?

One of the most persistent myths in any gym is that to build muscle a person must load up on dietary protein. In fact, the typical American diet includes much more protein than people need, whether or not they're seeking to increase muscle mass. Getting too much protein can be dangerous. High-protein diets produce excess nitrogen in the blood. This leads to a high acid condition. The body's response is to neutralize the acidity by leaching calcium from the bones, then excreting it in the urine. This process, if carried out over a lifetime, can be a factor in causing osteoporosis. The typical American diet includes too much animal protein. Animal protein, especially beef, pork, egg yolks, poultry with the skin, and cheese, is accompanied by unhealthy levels of fat and cholesterol—bad news for your heart and your weight.

How much protein is enough? Active people should be eating no more than 1.5–2.0 grams of protein per kilogram (2.2 pounds) of body weight, per day, or about 20 to 25% of total daily calories. Good sources of lean protein are egg whites, fish, fat-free dairy products, beans and other legumes, and white-meat poultry minus the skin.

Since we recommend seafood as a source of dietary protein, we'll list for you what we consider the three best sources, based on their percentage of calories from fat. They are cod, sole (flounder), and tuna (packed in water). All these are high in Omega-3 fatty acids, which may help to reverse heart disease. Cod is the lowest in percent calories from fat (7%), sole is second with 12%, and tuna is third with 16% of its calories from fat. All three are considered very low fat sources of animal protein.

Fiber

Getting plenty of fiber in your diet makes it easier to maintain a healthy (and shapely) body weight, and helps prevent diabetes, colon cancer, and heart disease. People need about 25 to 35 grams of fiber from food sources each day. Fresh fruits and vegetables, legumes (beans, peas, lentils), and whole grains are excellent sources of fiber.

To make your shopping easier, here is a list of some good sources of dietary fiber:

- Bran cereals: ½ cup has 6–14 grams (depending on brand)
- Baked beans: 8 grams per ½ cup
- Kidney or lima beans: 7 grams per ½ cup
- Broccoli or brussels sprouts: 7 grams per cup
- Fresh corn: 7 grams per ear
- Apples: 4 grams each
- Sweet potatoes: 4 grams per medium-size sweet potato
- Brown rice: 3 grams per ⅔ cup serving

- Bananas: 3 grams each
- Oranges: 3 grams each
- Peaches: 3 grams each
- Whole wheat tortillas: 3 grams each
- Tomatoes: 2 grams each

If you eat a balanced diet from natural food sources, including fruits, grains, and vegetables, your fiber consumption is probably adequate. Unless you're having problems with regularity, there's no need to go out of your way to supplement your diet with fiber foods such as bran. It is possible to eat too much fiber; fiber binds with calcium in the stomach, thereby reducing the amount of calcium that is absorbed. Women especially need plenty of calcium to guard against osteoporosis in their later years.

Phytochemicals

You may have heard or read about a group of compounds called phytochemicals. They are a new variety of natural compounds recently discovered in fruits and vegetables. They have no nutritive value, but it is believed these compounds may work to help protect the body from disease.

A diet containing lots of fruits and vegetables is the best source of phytochemicals; it is not possible at this point to get the benefits of phytochemicals through supplements. Fruits and vegetables also contain vitamins, antioxidants, minerals, and fiber, all of which promote good health and help prevent disease.

The chart here provides a listing of the top ten disease-fighting foods and the chemicals they contain that make them so effective in warding off disease. Most of the ingredients given are disease-preventing "phytochemicals." Beta-carotene and vitamin C are antioxidant vitamins. Fortunately, none of these valuable substances are destroyed by cooking, canning, freezing, or other processing of food.

Disease Fighting Foods

Food	Active Ingredient(s)
Broccoli	Sulforaphane, Beta-carotene, Indol-carbinol
Tomatoes	Lycopene
Spinach	Glutathione
Oranges	Bioflavonoid, Vitamin C
Garlic	Allicin
Apples	Elagic acid
Soybeans	Genistein
Carrots	Beta-carotene
Hot Red Peppers	Capsaicin
Green Tea	Catechin

Minerals

Minerals activate your body's enzymes, which are necessary for metabolism. They aid in the transfer of nerve impulses, muscle contraction, body growth and development, and water balance. Minerals are especially important for people who exercise, because they maintain the body's electrolyte (mineral) balance.

The major minerals are calcium, phosphorus, magnesium, and sulfur. Important electrolytes are sodium chloride and potassium. The trace minerals, needed in smaller quantities but still vital to health, are iron, zinc, iodide, copper, manganese, fluoride, chromium, selenium, and molybdenum.

If you eat a variety of wholesome foods, you don't have to worry about getting enough of these nutrients. (The one possible exception, especially for women, is calcium, which we'll discuss next.) The best way to meet your mineral needs is through a balanced diet. High-quality multi-mineral supplements, in moderation, won't hurt. However, taking some individual mineral supplements can greatly diminish the absorption and metabolism of other minerals. Again, this concern need not worry those who take calcium supplements to meet their daily needs.

Calcium—A Major Mineral

Calcium is important in building teeth and strong bones, and in preventing osteoporosis (thinning of the bones) as we grow older. To

Best Food Sources of Dietary Calcium

Calcium (mg.)	Foods
400	plain yogurt, 1 cup
370	sardines
300	milk (all types), 1 cup
290	enriched orange juice, 1 cup
270	Swiss cheese, 1 oz.
225	salmon, 3 oz.
205	cheddar cheese, 1 oz.
200	turnip greens, 1 cup cooked
175	ice cream or ice milk, 1 cup
165	fortified oatmeal, 1 pack
150	cottage cheese, 1 cup
150–250	fortified cereal, ¾ cup
140	canned baked beans, 1 cup
115	tofu, 2 oz.
95	kale, 1 cup cooked
70	broccoli, 1 cup cooked

make sure you don't join the millions of Americans with osteoporosis, get plenty of calcium in your diet.

The recommended daily allowances of calcium for various age groups are: for ages 11 through 24, 1200 mg.; over 25 years, 800 mg.; women over 50/men over 65, 1500–1800 mg.

Calcium requirements can be met through diet alone, or through diet and supplements.

Vitamins

Vitamins are found in all foods. They help regulate the metabolism and protect the body from disease. If you eat a wide variety of nutritious foods, you shouldn't have to worry about supplementing your diet with vitamin pills.

Water

Water is found in fruits, vegetables, and liquids. It is the most essential nutrient of all. You can't survive more than a few days without it. It transports nutrients, regulates body heat, and aids in digestion. Drink plenty of water throughout the day, especially while you're working out!

The Importance of a Low-Fat Diet

If your goal is to lose body fat, then cut down on your overall daily calorie intake, especially calories from fat.

If you want to maintain your current body weight, the number of calories you need to eat depends on how much exercise you get. But the appropriate generalized formula following will give you a rough idea of the calories you need to eat per day to maintain your current body weight.

Adult women: Multiply current body weight by 10, then add weight to that value.

Example: 130 pounds × 10 = 1300
+ 130 lbs. = 1430 calories per day

Adult men: Multiply current body weight by 10, then add double your weight to this value.

Example: 180 pounds × 10 = 1800
+ 360 pounds = 2160 calories per day

Make sure your diet always gives you at least 1200 calories a day. Any number below that and your body's metabolic rate (the rate at which you burn calories) will start to slow down. You don't want that to happen—you want your body to burn calories faster and more efficiently. To keep your metabolism revved up, eat about 55% of total daily calories from carbohydrates (preferably complex carbs—emphasize fruits and vegetables), eat 20–25% from fat (no more than 7% from saturated fat), and get 20–25% from protein (vegetable and low-fat sources are best). When you eat this way, your body produces enough energy so that you will have the stamina to exercise. After a short conditioning period, exercise itself produces energy.

There's a popular myth these days that if you eat a low-fat diet, you can eat all the carbohydrates you want and still not gain weight. Unfortunately, it's not true. If you eat too much in general (and don't burn enough calories through exercise), you won't lose weight and you might gain weight.

Calories are units of energy which are used as fuel for your body. If you put more fuel in your body than the body can use, the body has a mechanism for storing this fuel—it's called fat. So even if you eat a high-carb, low-fat diet, the number of calories going in still must not exceed the number of calories going out, if you want to lose weight.

However, it certainly helps to eat a diet low in fat and high in complex carbohydrates. Fat in food is stored as body fat more easily than carbohydrates are. Simple carbs, such as refined flour, many processed foods, sugars, sweets, and fruit juices, elevate blood glucose and insulin levels, and this process also stimulates fat storage. On the other hand, complex carbohydrates actually stimulate the cells of your body to burn calories faster. Complex carbs include whole grains, brown rice, potatoes, vegetables, and beans.

Complex carbohydrates cannot add directly to body fat. In order for your body to store their energy, you have to chemically convert it to fat. This is not an easy task, and the conversion process "wastes" 23% of the calories contained in that food. When you eat fat, the task is much easier and only uses up 3% of the calories in that food.

Because there is more fiber in complex carbs and fewer calories per gram (4 calories compared to 9 in a gram of fat), carbs are more filling and have fewer calories. That means that if your diet is high in complex carbohydrates, you can get away with eating more in general! Remember, though, if you want to lose weight, not maintain it, you'll probably have to cut down on total calories, or exercise more.

If you want to be trim and fit, a good diet coupled with regular aerobic exercise and weight training is the name of the game. Consistent exercise is the key factor in teaching your body to be an efficient fat burner and not a fat storer!

Finally, be aware of "insulin resistance" and its relation to diet. The job of insulin is to transport sugar from the bloodstream into the cells, where it is needed for energy. Simply put, insulin resistance means that a person's insulin is not doing its job properly. If your insulin isn't effective, your pancreas will secrete more and more insulin. That can create problems—people with high insulin levels are at greater risk of developing high blood pressure, heart disease, and diabetes.

High insulin levels usually occur in people who are overweight. Because of their excess fat, the receptor sites on their body's cells don't recognize insulin very easily, and more insulin must be secreted in order for the hormone to do its job. How can you tell if you're insulin resistant? The best indicators are high triglyceride levels, low HDL (the good kind of cholesterol), and being overweight.

The bottom line: if you're overweight, you probably have some degree of insulin resistance. Exercise and lose weight, and your insulin levels should return to normal. Stay fat and you have a good chance of becoming diabetic.

Nutrition Reminders

The 1995 dietary guidelines according to the U.S. Departments of Agriculture and Health and Human Services are as follows:

1. Eat a wide variety of foods.
2. Balance the food you eat with physical activity to maintain or improve your weight.
3. Choose a diet low in fat, saturated fat, and cholesterol.
4. Choose a diet with plenty of grains, vegetables, and fruits.
5. Choose a diet moderate in sugars.
6. Choose a diet moderate in salt and sodium.
7. If you drink alcoholic beverages, do so in moderation.

Remember, a healthy diet is made up of grains, legumes, fruits and vegetables, nonfat dairy products, and small amounts of animal proteins (seafood, egg whites, skinless poultry, or meat.) Make water your beverage of choice, and drink plenty of it throughout the day.

Chapter 4

Shape-Training Exercises

Thighs and Buttocks

The thighs and buttocks are the two hardest areas of the body to train. The muscles involved are the largest in your body; it requires a lot of energy to train them hard enough to make a difference.

There is also the knee tracking factor. The knees have to track correctly in order to avoid injuring them. Knees are a hinge joint and should move back and forth in only one plane of motion. It takes a certain amount of muscle strength and body awareness to keep the knees properly aligned. Knees tend to turn out or cave in.

Finally, there is the lower back to consider. Almost all leg and buttocks exercises involve the erectors or lower-back muscles, either as prime movers or stabilizers. Often the weaker erector muscles prevent us from working our leg and buttocks muscles to full capacity. Those who begin with relatively undeveloped lower-back muscles will find they must ease up on some of the lower-body exercises until their backs are strong enough to handle the load.

Thus, training the lower body is not only more physically demanding than other muscle groups, but also requires a higher degree of mental focus in order to prevent injury.

If you carefully follow the directions for each exercise, your lower-back muscles and knee joints will be protected and not at risk for injury.

Knee Extension

(works quadriceps—front of upper leg)

Starting Position Follow directions on the equipment and adjust it to fit your body. The roller pads should be even with your ankle bones. Feet are relaxed, toes pointing straight ahead.

Movement

A. Exhale, and straighten out your knees, bringing your legs almost parallel to the floor.

B. Inhale, and slowly lower your legs four-fifths of the way down.

Notes

- Don't kick your legs up or drop them down. Strive for controlled, even movements.
- Don't lock the knees at the top of the movement (avoid hyperextending the knees).
- Lower your legs only four-fifths of the way down to avoid hyperflexion (over-stretching) of the knees.

> CAUTION: If you have knee problems, you may not be able to do knee extensions. If your knees themselves hurt when doing the exercise or afterwards, lighten the load. If your knees still hurt with any amount of weight, you should probably avoid this exercise completely.

Leg Curl
(works hamstring—back of upper leg)

Starting Position Follow directions on the equipment and adjust it to fit your body. The roller pads should be resting on the area between your Achilles tendons and your lower calf muscles.

Movement

A. Exhale as you bend your knees, bringing your feet toward your buttocks.

B. Inhale as you slowly lower your legs four-fifths of the way down.

Notes

- Don't lower your legs any farther than four-fifths of the way down, to avoid hyperextension of the knees.
- Strive for a controlled, even movement.

Advanced Variation When your knees are fully flexed, lift your thighs off the bench by squeezing your buttocks muscles. Do not perform this variation if you have lower-back problems.

> CAUTION: If you have a weak lower back or lower-back problems, you may not be able to do this exercise. If your lower back hurts while doing the exercise or afterward, lighten the load.

Squat

(works thighs, buttocks and lower back)

Squats are a high-risk exercise and must be performed with caution (see box on opposite page).

Starting Position Step under the bar and place the bar across your upper trapezius muscles (between your shoulders). Step back away from the rack. Stand with your feet hip-width apart, toes pointing straight ahead. If you're very tall, you may have to position your feet wider than hip width and your feet may have to be turned out slightly. Knees should be relaxed, not locked, your back straight (allowing for the natural curve), and your chin level. Look up with your eyes only.

Movement

A. Inhale, lowering your body as if you were sitting down in a chair. Go down until your thighs are parallel to the floor (if you're able). Your shoulders should never go farther forward than mid-thigh.

B. Exhale as you straighten your body, pressing your heels into the floor and squeezing your buttocks as you do so.

Notes

- Don't allow your knees to come together.
- Keep your feet flat on the floor throughout the exercise.
- Strive for controlled, even movements.
- During the lowering phase of the lift, don't allow your shoulders and the barbell to go any farther forward than above the middle of your thighs.
- At the start of the movement, your hips should tilt back slightly, as if you were sitting down in a chair.

CAUTION: If you have lower-back or knee problems, you may not be able to do squats. To try them, do the exercise as described but *don't* lower your body all the way down. If you have tight Achilles tendons, the same limited range of motion applies.

Variation *Front Squat* Feet and knees are together, as shown at left. The bar rests across the front of your deltoids and chest in a cross-arm position. This variation targets the quads (front of upper legs) more than does a standard squat. The front squat is not for beginners; it requires a good sense of balance and front shoulder development.

Standard Dip

(works thighs and buttocks)

Starting Position Step under the bar and place the bar across your upper traps (trapezius muscles), with your feet hip-width apart. Then step forward and place one foot on an elevated surface. You will be on the ball of the back foot, which is extended behind you. Position yourself so that the front knee will be directly over the ankle at the lowest point of the movement. Both feet are pointed straight ahead.

Movement

A. Inhale as you lower your body by bending the front knee and pressing the back knee toward the floor.

B. Exhale, lifting back to the starting position.

Notes

- Stay on the ball of the back foot throughout the entire exercise.
- Strive for controlled and even movements.
- At the bottom of the movement, make sure your front knee and ankle are aligned.

> CAUTION: If you have knee problems, you may not be able to do this exercise.

One-Leg Dip

(works thighs and buttocks)

This is an advanced exercise because it requires considerable balance and coordination.

Starting Position Step under the bar and place it across your upper traps (trapezius muscles). Place the top of one foot and ankle across a bench behind you. The other leg will be in front of your body. Position this leg so that the knee is directly over the ankle at the lowest point of the exercise. This foot is pointing straight ahead.

Movement

A. Inhale, and lower your body by bending both your knees.

B. Exhale, and lift back up to the starting position.

Notes

- Strive for controlled, even movements.
- Keep the front knee and ankle aligned at the lowest point of the exercise.
- The front foot remains pointed straight ahead throughout the exercise.

> CAUTION: If you have knee problems, you may not be able to do this exercise.

Lunge

(works thighs and buttocks)

Starting Position Step under the bar and place it across your upper traps. Step back from the rack and stand with your feet hip-width apart. Both feet are pointing straight ahead.

Movement

A. Inhale as you lunge forward, simultaneously pressing the back knee toward the floor.

B. Exhale, coming back to the starting position.

Notes

- Lunges require a degree of agility. If you find the movement difficult, stick with dips until you develop more body awareness.
- Strive for controlled and even movements.
- When you step back after each lunge, step into a hip-width stance.
- Position yourself so that the lunging knee is directly over the ankle at the lowest point of the movement.

CAUTION: If you have knee problems, you may not be able to do this exercise.

Step-Up

(works thighs and buttocks)

Starting Position Face a flat bench with a set of dumbbells in your hands, or with a barbell across your traps.

Movement

A. Exhale as you step up onto the bench with your right foot, then immediately step up with the left foot.

B. Inhale, and step down (backwards) with your right foot, followed by your left.

Notes

- Always begin your step down on the same foot with which you began the step up.
- If you're holding dumbbells, don't allow your arms to swing.
- Place your entire foot on the bench you're stepping onto.
- Do this exercise slowly to avoid losing your balance and falling.

> CAUTION: If you have knee problems, you may not be able to do step-ups.

Adduction

(works the inner thighs)

Starting Position Follow directions on the equipment and adjust it to fit your body. Hip and inner thigh flexibility are factors that must be considered in this adjustment.

Movement

A. Exhale, and squeeze your legs all the way together.

B. Inhale, and slowly open your legs four-fifths of the way back to the starting position.

Notes

- Don't allow your legs to jerk open. Strive for controlled, even movements.
- Don't allow your buttocks to lift off the bench when squeezing your legs together.

CAUTION: If you have a weak lower back or lower-back problems, you may not be able to do this exercise.

Hip Extension on Knee-Extension Apparatus

(works the buttocks)

Starting Position If your gym has a hip-extension apparatus, follow the directions on the equipment. However, many gyms don't have such equipment. In that case, you can use the knee-extension apparatus to work your buttocks. Adjust the equipment to fit your body. Facing toward the back rest of the apparatus, rest the front of your hip against the front of the seat pad. To stabilize your lower back, grab the seat or back rest wherever it feels comfortable. Place your standing leg wide and out of the way of your working leg. The back of the working leg is placed in front of the roller pad, right at the area between the Achilles tendon and the lower-calf muscle.

Movement

A. Exhale, lifting your leg up behind you by contracting your buttocks muscles.

B. Inhale, slowly lowering your leg to the starting position.

Notes

- Keep the hip of the working leg pressed against the bench.
- Strive for controlled, even movements.

Specific Stretches for the Leg Muscles

Leg Stretch 1 – Cat Stretch

Stand with your knees bent, hands on top of your thighs, shoulders dropped and pulled back, head up, and back gently arched. Hold and breathe for 20 seconds. Next, slowly round your lower back, roll your shoulders forwards and drop your head. Hold and breathe for 20 seconds.

Leg Stretch 2 – Quad Stretch

Stand on left leg, balancing by holding on to something with your left hand. Reach back with your right hand, take hold of your right ankle, and pull your leg up behind you as far as you can, while leaning forward slightly.

Leg Stretch 3 – Glute and Hamstring Stretch

Extend left leg forward and flex left foot. Bend your right leg and rest your hands on front of right thigh. Lean into the stretch by bending forward at the waist and pushing your buttocks back. Hold and breathe for 20 seconds. Repeat with other leg.

Chest
(Pectoralis Muscles)

When you train your chest muscles you also work the deltoid (shoulder) muscles. Please be extra careful when performing chest exercises, because the deltoids are vulnerable and easily injured. If you exceed the proper range of motion, you could hurt your shoulder.

Chest exercises with free weights are performed while lying on your back. When lowering the weight, never lower the elbows more than approximately two inches below the shoulders. If you do lower the weight beyond this point, you're crossing an "anatomical barrier." You'll place extreme stress on the deltoid muscle and the shoulder joint, without further benefit to the chest muscles.

Never hyperextend (or "lock") your elbows at the end of a lift. This rule applies to other joints also, and to all weight-lifting exercises. Locking the joints transfers the resistance (weight) from the working muscle and onto the joints, which in turn puts undue pressure on the bones and connective tissue. Hyper-extending your joints will not increase the benefit of the exercise to the muscle, and may lead to injury.

When performing exercises for the chest, try to keep the shoulder blades pulled together. This may not be easy at first if you're a beginner. Retracting the scapulae in this way opens and expands the pectoral plate (chest muscles) and shortens the distance the weight has to travel. This increases the amount of power you can exert during the lift.

Avoid arching your lower back. This is a general rule and should be applied to all lifts. Arching is cheating, and when you cheat two things happen (or don't happen). First, you increase the likelihood of injury. When you arch your back, you're using your whole upper body instead of focusing the effort on your chest muscles. The result can be a back strain. Secondly, arching uses leverage to lift the weight, and that cuts into your true strength gains. Keep your back flat (allowing for your natural curve) by placing your feet on the bench or flat on the floor close to the bench. Without the added artificial advantage of arching, you may have to reduce the amount of weight you're lifting, but you'll get more training benefits and see quicker improvement in your chest and shoulders.

If you have a shoulder injury, you may want to avoid some or all of the chest exercises, particularly the wide-grip variations. Start with lower weights and be sensitive to which exercises cause pain in your shoulder.

To learn how to prevent and treat exercise injuries, see those sections in Chapter 2.

Spotting, when using heavy weights or learning proper technique, helps to avoid injury.

Bench Press – Standard Grip

This is the best overall exercise for developing muscle and building strength in the pectoralis (chest) muscles.

Starting Position Lie on the bench, with your feet either on the bench or flat on the floor, the bar over the bridge of your nose, and your hands 2½ to 3 feet apart. Retract the scapulae (pull your shoulder blades together), and lift the bar up and out from the rack. If you're a beginner, don't focus on pulling your shoulder blades together; just allow your shoulder blades to move freely.

Movement

A. Inhale as you slowly lower the bar toward your chest, just over your sternum, as shown below.

CAUTION: When doing wide-grip bench presses, be careful not to use too wide a grip. If you do, you will be placing all the resistance on the anterior shoulder muscles and this can lead to injury. Although it is difficult to set a general rule, you should be safe as long as you don't angle your hands out from the elbows by more than five inches.

Use lighter weights when first experimenting with this variation, and be sure that your hands are positioned so that you feel the effort in your chest, not in your shoulders.

B. Exhale as you push the bar up and back in a very slight arc toward the rack.

When doing incline and decline presses (see Variation), you will lower the bar to a point over the nipple line, and push straight up.

Variation The bench press is a very versatile exercise; there are four ways you can alter the effect. Your grip can be narrowed to target the inner chest, or widened to work the outer chest and deltoids. To focus on the upper part of the pectoral plate, use an incline bench. Use a decline bench in order to target the lower pecs.

Notes

- Don't arch your back.
- Don't let the elbows drop any lower than approximately two inches below the shoulders.
- Don't lock your elbows at the top of the movement.
- Squeeze your chest muscles at the top of the movement.

Low-Pulley Cable Fly

This exercise is great for shaping the lower and outer portions of your chest.
Starting Position Stand with your feet hip-width apart, back straight, pelvis in a neutral position. With your hands facing forward, take a pulley handle in each hand, allowing the resistance of the weight to extend your arms out at your sides. This will place your hands about 20 inches beyond your legs. Your elbows should be slightly bent.

Movement
A. Exhale and slowly raise both pulleys toward the front of your body, in an upward-curving movement, until your hands are at eye level.
B. Inhale and reverse the movement, returning to starting position. Do so slowly and don't allow the cables to jerk your arms.
Notes
- Keep your pelvis neutral throughout the exercise.
- Keep your back straight.
- Keep the elbows slightly flexed.
- Squeeze your chest muscles at the top of the movement.

Dumbbell Press – Flat Bench

Starting Position Lie on the bench, feet on the bench or flat on the floor. Hold a dumbbell in each hand, palms facing forward. Arms are straight up over the chest, elbows slightly flexed. Retract the scapulae.

Movement

A. Inhale as you slowly lower the dumbbells to approximately shoulder level.

B. Exhale as you press the weights straight up to the starting position.

Notes

- Don't arch your back.
- Keep the dumbbells directly over your chest, not over your face or stomach.
- Don't bend your wrists.
- At the bottom of the movement, don't lower your elbows any farther than approximately two inches below your shoulders.
- Squeeze your chest muscles at the top of the movement.
- Don't lock your elbows at the top of the movement.

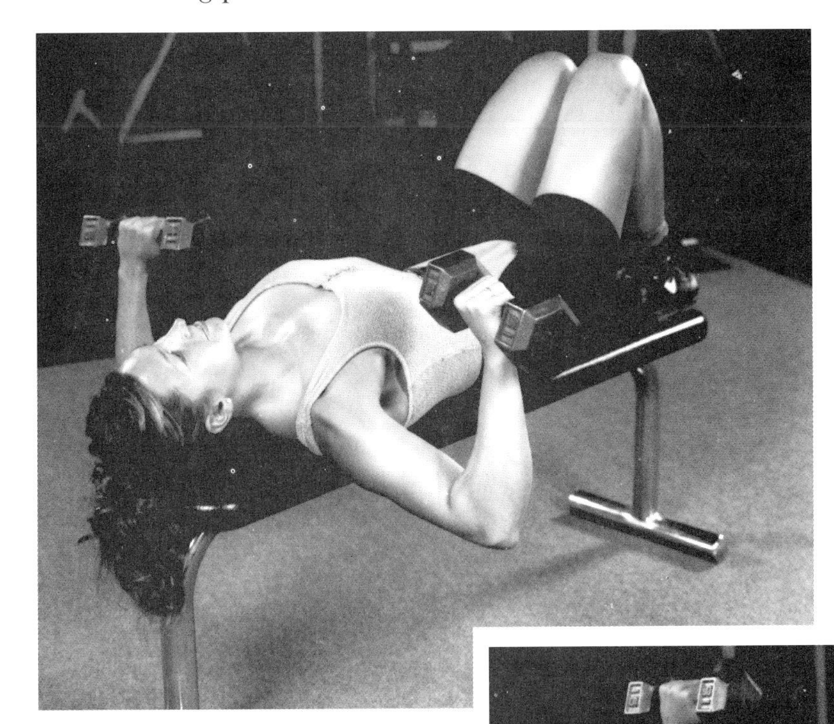

Variation Use a 45-degree incline bench to focus on the upper pecs and a decline bench to target the lower pectoral muscles.

Fly – Incline Bench

Doing the dumbbell fly on an incline bench is effective for specially targeting the upper and outer portions of the pectoral plate.

Starting Position Lie on the bench, feet flat on the floor. Hold a dumbbell in each hand, palms facing forward (toward your feet) or palms facing each other. Arms are straight up over the chest, elbows are slightly flexed. Retract the scapulae.

Movement

A. As you inhale slowly, open your arms until your hands are approximately two inches below your shoulders.

B. Follow a semicircular path, as if you were hugging a giant tree, back to the starting position. As always, exhale during the lift.

Notes

- Keep the dumbbells in line with the chest (do not move them in the direction of your head or your feet).
- Don't bend your wrists.
- Don't arch your back.
- Keep your elbows slightly flexed throughout the exercise.
- Squeeze your chest muscles at the top of the movement.

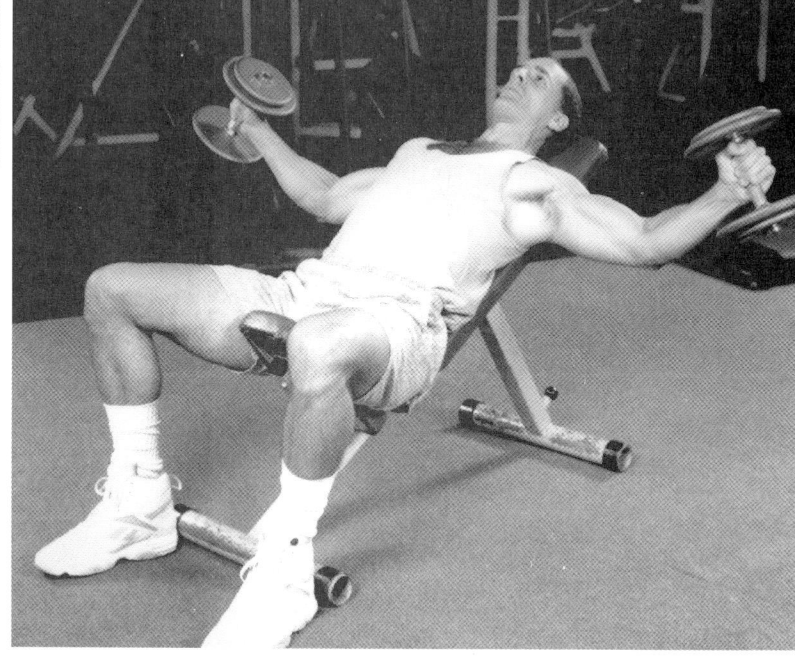

Variation Use a flat bench to focus on the overall pecs (feet may be on floor or on bench), and a decline bench to target the outer/lower chest muscles.

Pullover

The pullover is effective for targeting the inner chest.

Starting Position Lie on the bench, feet on the bench or flat on the floor. Hold a single dumbbell at arms length (elbows slightly flexed) above your chest, with both hands, palms up, wrapped around one end of the dumbbell.

Movement

A. Allowing the elbows to bend only slightly, lower the dumbbell slowly toward the floor (over your head) until your arms are parallel with your ears. Inhale during this part of the movement.

B. Keeping the arms almost straight, slowly raise the dumbbell back up to the starting position (exhale).

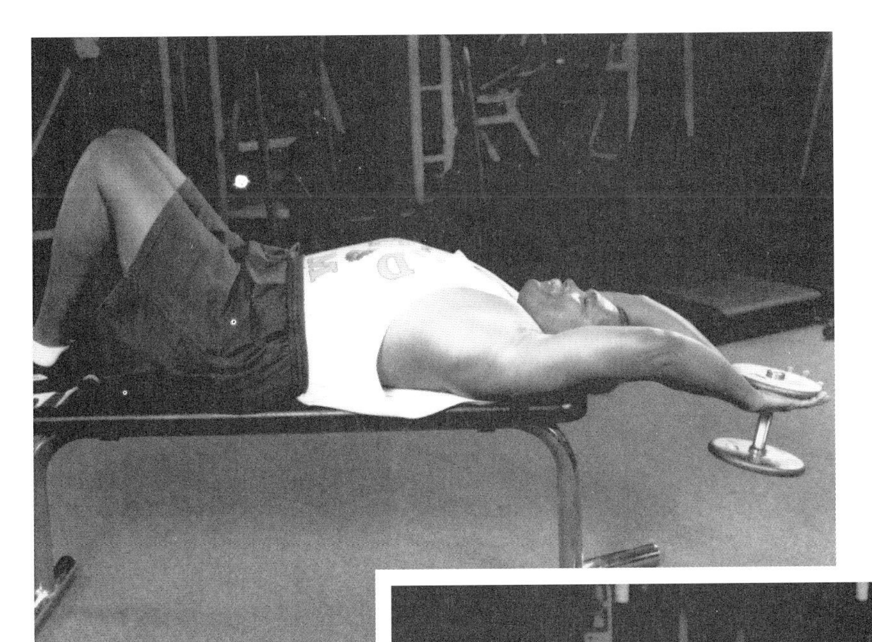

Notes

- Squeeze your chest muscles at the top of the movement.
- Don't arch your back.
- Don't lower your arms any farther than ear height.
- Don't bend your elbows any more than slightly at any point in the lift.

Variation In place of a dumbbell, use a bar as your weight. Use a narrow grip to target the inner chest, and a wider grip to target the outer chest.

CAUTION: Don't use too wide a grip or you won't be using the chest muscles at all and you'll be placing the deltoid muscles at risk for injury.

Standard Push-Up

Push-ups are an all-time great exercise for the chest, shoulders, and arms. Although some prefer the use of push-up bars, this exercise requires no equipment and allows you to get a good chest workout even when you don't have access to a gym or equipment.

Starting Position Lie facedown on the floor. Position your hands beside your shoulders. With your legs together, flex your feet so that the balls of your feet are on the floor.

Movement

A. Exhale, while keeping your torso straight, and push your body up until your arms are fully extended (don't lock your elbows).

B. Inhale and slowly lower yourself until your nose touches the floor.

Notes

- Be sure to keep your torso straight (this helps to contract your abdominal muscles).
- Don't lock your elbows.
- Keep your elbows near your sides.
- Inexpensive push-up bars are recommended, for all varieties of push-ups, to take the pressure off your wrists. When using push-up bars, you should no longer go down until your nose touches the floor. Instead, stop at the point where your shoulders are about one inch lower than your elbows.

Variations

- Most, but not all, women find that push-ups from the knees are sufficient to effectively exercise the chest muscles. This variation is performed exactly the same as a standard push-up, only instead of lifting from your feet, you're lifting from your knees as shown.
- To emphasize the inner chest and triceps, do push-ups with your hands close together.
- To target the outer chest and deltoids, do push-ups with your hands placed about 8 inches out from your shoulders.
- To make the push-up more difficult, place your feet on a stool, chair, or bench.

CAUTION: The last two variations above (wide-hand position and elevated feet) both place a lot of stress on the shoulder muscles. Be sure your deltoids are sufficiently developed to handle this extra workload.

Pect Deck

(works chest and front shoulders—the anterior deltoids)

Starting Position Adjust the seat so your arms are straight out from your shoulders.

Movement

A. Exhale as you push your arms together until the equipment pads nearly touch.

B. Inhale as you slowly open your arms, without jerking the weight, until your arms are flush with your chest, no farther.

Note When returning the weights to the starting position, don't allow your arms to go any farther back than the shoulders.

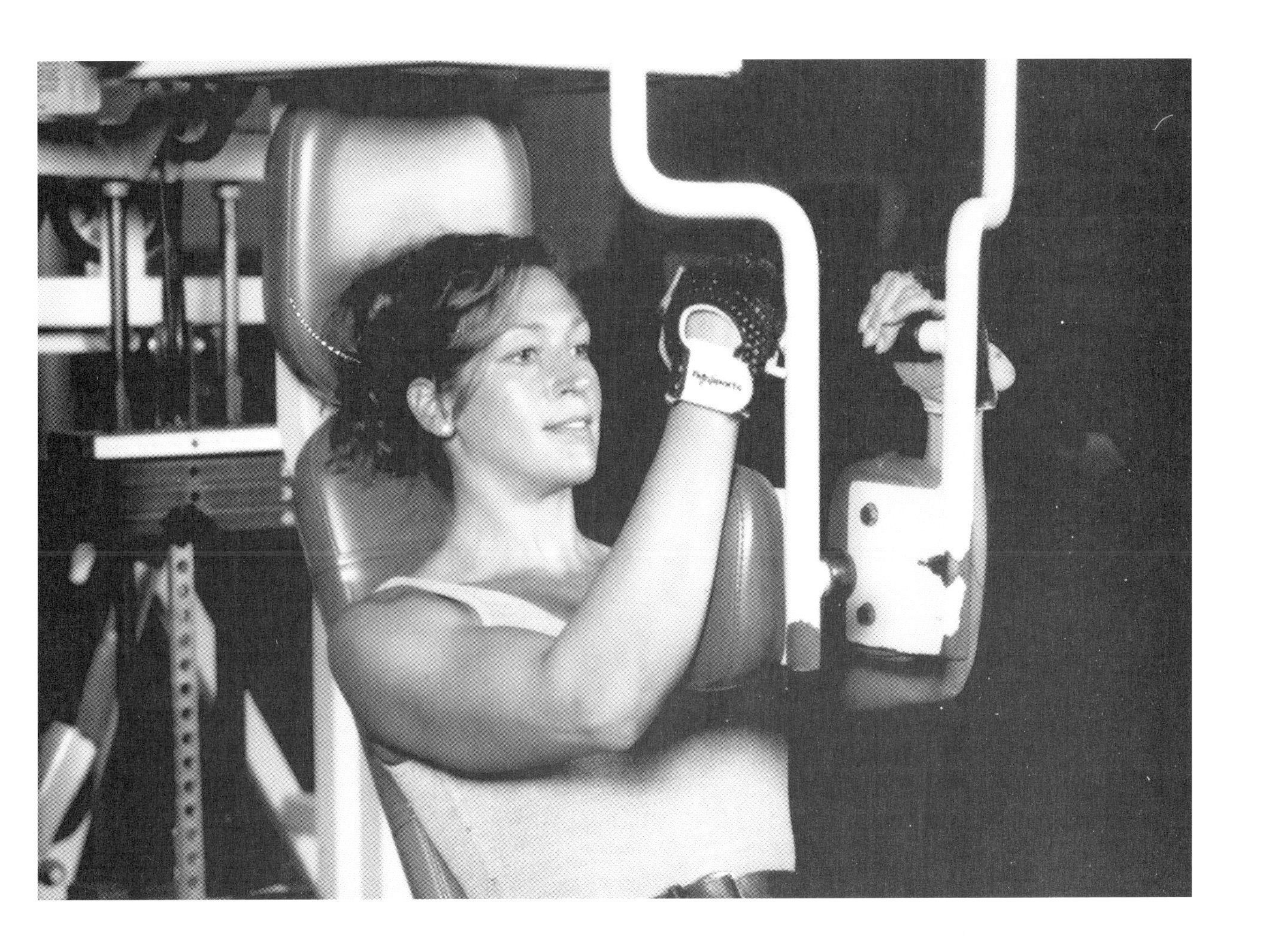

Specific Stretches for Chest Muscles

Chest Stretch 1

Interlace your hands behind your head and pull your elbows back as far as you can. Hold and breathe for 20 seconds.

Chest Stretch 2

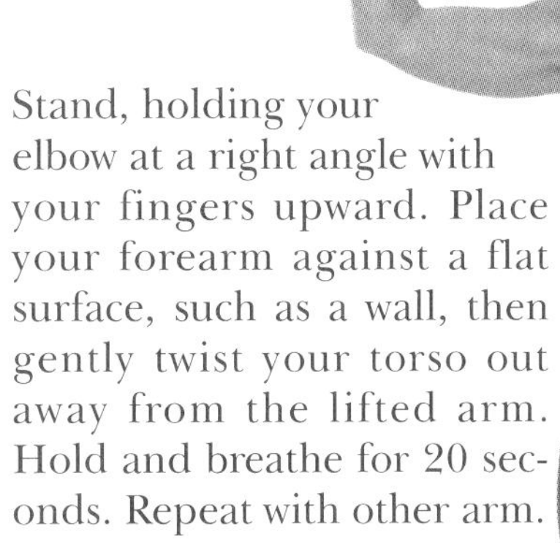

Stand, holding your elbow at a right angle with your fingers upward. Place your forearm against a flat surface, such as a wall, then gently twist your torso out away from the lifted arm. Hold and breathe for 20 seconds. Repeat with other arm.

The Back

To train the back effectively, you must be aware of the great variety of muscles that make up this area of your body.

There are the smaller muscles in the upper back—the rhomboids, infraspinatus, and teres major. The upper and mid back also contain the larger, more powerful trapezius ("traps") and latissimus dorsi ("lats") muscles. Finally there are the lower-back or erector muscles. These are usually the weakest of all the back muscles, and the most vulnerable to injury.

We divide the back muscles into 4 quadrants. The upper-back muscles make up one group, the muscles of the lower back another. The lats, which shape the outer back, are the third quadrant, and the middle and lower traps make up the middle back.

The large, powerful lats and upper traps (latissimus dorsi and trapezius) are the easiest muscles to train, simply because they are so big. The smaller muscles of the upper back—the rhomboids, teres major, and infraspinatus—and the lower and middle traps (middle back) are harder to isolate.

Shaping your back proportionally means bringing out these smaller muscle groups as well as the lats and upper traps. In order to effectively train the smaller muscles, you must follow specific refined movement patterns, otherwise the lats and traps do all the work and reap all the training benefits. The exercises that follow give careful consideration to these movement patterns. If you've had experience training the back, these exercises may be slightly different from what you're used to.

The erectors (lower back) are a notoriously weak muscle group; in many people they are out of shape or even injured. Close attention is paid below to correct (safe) body mechanics in all the exercises, but especially in those that focus on the lower-back muscles.

All the back muscles are integral to developing and maintaining good posture. Each muscle has to be trained in conjunction with the others. In this way you maintain muscle balance and avoid overtraining a particular muscle.

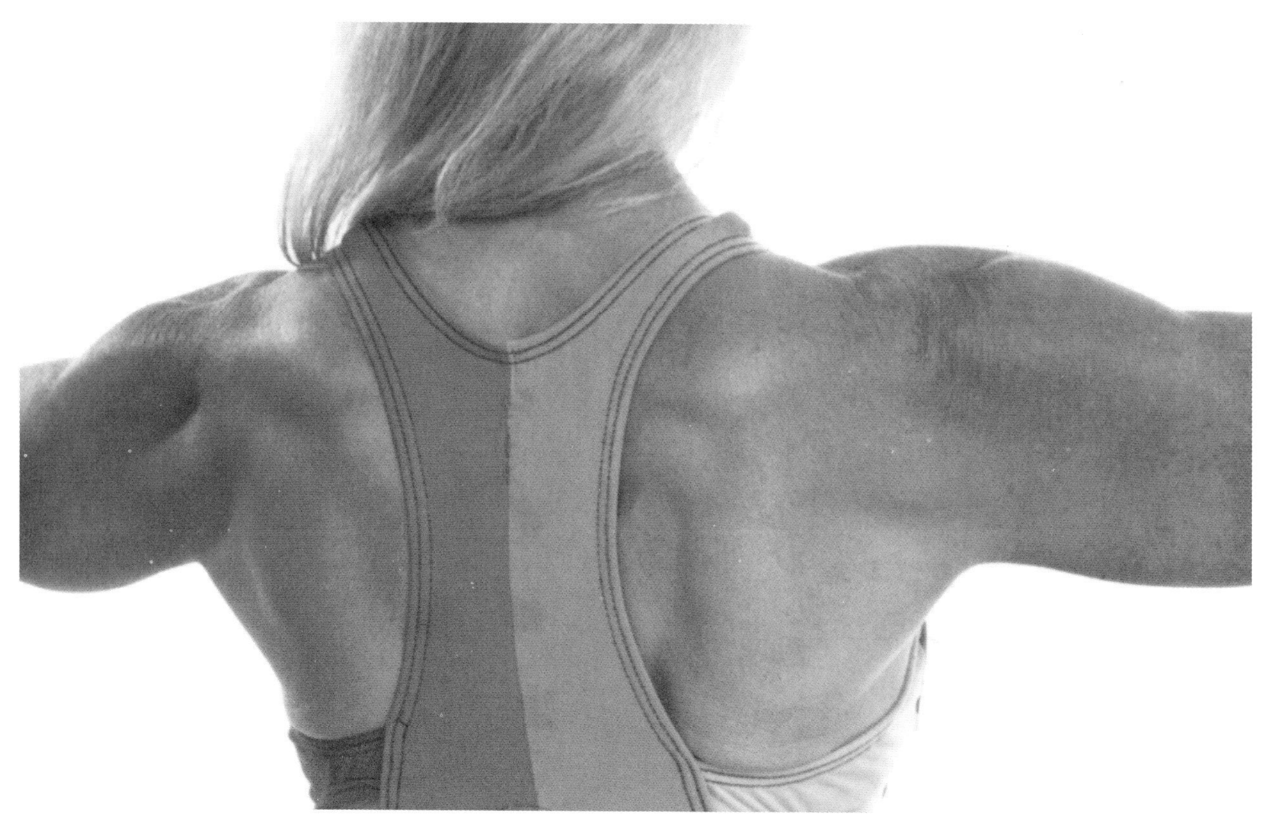

Standard Lat

The most advanced form of lat (latissimus dorsi) pulls is to the rear of the head. All lat pull-down exercises, whether pulling to the front or back of the body, generally work to widen the back.

Starting Position Take the bar in a medium grip, palms facing forward. Sit on the bench so the bar will come down behind your head without your having to lean forward at the waist. Feet are flat on the floor, knees are at a right angle. Elevate your shoulder blades. (This is an exercise refinement that automatically engages the smaller upper-back muscles as you start the working phase of the lift.)

Movement

A. Exhale and depress your shoulder blades as you slowly pull the bar down behind your head, toward your upper traps. (If you're pulling the bar down in front of your head as a variation, bring it down to your upper chest.) Your elbows should pull straight down to the floor, and remain pointing toward the floor throughout both phases of the lift. This exercise refinement takes out most of the external shoulder rotation from the movement, and makes the exercise much safer to do.

B. Inhale as you slowly return the bar to the starting position, elevating your shoulder blades at the end of the return.

Notes

- Don't arch your back.
- Keep your knees at a right angle to stabilize your back.
- Elbows should point straight down to the floor throughout the exercise.

Variations

- The grip variations and bar options used in back exercises are nearly endless. It's important to include a variety of bars and grips in your back routines. That way you'll be sure to target all the back muscles and you'll be able to isolate parts of the bigger back muscles as well. A wide grip targets the outer portion of the lats, a close grip the inner portion and some lower traps. A medium grip is best for working the lat muscles overall. You can hold the bar with an overhand or with an underhand grip.
- For variety, you can pull the bar down in front of your chest instead of behind your head, as shown below. Pulling to the front, in an underhand grip (palms toward you) is the safest, most effective method for beginners.
- Utilize all the bars available to you. They each work the back muscles a little differently. Variety, a key factor in long-term exercise adherence, keeps your workouts interesting and challenging.

CAUTION: If you have tight neck muscles or shoulder problems, perform all your lat pull-down exercises to the front of your body. That way you'll avoid straining the neck and protect the shoulders.

Seated Low-Pulley Cable Row

(works lats, middle back, and shoulder girdle)

Starting Position Take the rowing bar in your hands and push back into starting position by straightening your legs most of the way (your knees remain slightly flexed throughout the exercise). Your back is straight, chin level, and your shoulders are dropped.

Movement

A. Keeping your arms close to your body, exhale and slowly pull the bar toward your sternum. Don't lean back. As you're pulling the bar back, pull your shoulder blades together and expand (open up) your chest.

B. Inhale and slowly, without jerking the weight, return to the starting position. When you're finished with your set, carefully slide your whole body forward until the tension is off the cable and the plates are restacked. At no time in this exercise should you lean your body forward.

Notes

- Don't arch your back.
- Don't lean either forward or backward during the exercise—your back should remain straight.
- Keep your arms close to your body at all times.
- Bring the bar to your sternum.
- Knees remain slightly flexed throughout the exercise.

Variations

- The grip variations and bar options used in low-pulley rowing exercises are nearly endless. Variety, a key factor in long-term exercise adherence, keeps your workouts interesting and challenging. So utilize all the bars available; they each target the back muscles a little differently. However, in any one workout, once you've begun an exercise with a particular bar and grip, stick with that same bar and grip for all of your sets of that exercise.

- *One-Arm Seated Row* You can also perform a seated row with one arm at a time. In doing so, your torso slightly twists in the direction of that arm as you row the handle in toward your sternum. The mechanics of the rest of the body remain the same.

CAUTION: If you have a lower-back problem, this exercise is still safe to do *if* it is performed exactly as described. Do not lean your body forward as you return the weight to the starting position. If you do, you are putting your back at high risk for injury.

Bent-Over One-Arm Row

(works lats primarily)

Secondarily, this exercise also works the tricep, shoulder girdle, and rear deltoid muscles. It tends to "thicken" rather than widen the lat muscles. Lats developed in this way help correct bad posture by fortifying the upper torso.

Starting Position Place one hand, elbow slightly flexed, and the corresponding knee on a flat bench. Take a dumbbell in the other hand, palm turned toward the body. Shoulders are squared, abs tight, back is flat.

Movement

A. Exhale and slowly row the dumbbell straight up until it's beside your chest. Keep your arm close to your body throughout the exercise.

> CAUTION: All three of these variations require a strong lower back because only the back is used to stabilize the body. Make sure the back muscles are sufficiently trained to handle this added workload.

B. Inhale and slowly, without dropping the shoulder, lower the weight to the starting position.

Notes

- Don't arch your back.
- Keep your torso still and your abs tight.
- Look straight down at the floor throughout the exercise.
- Supporting elbow remains slightly flexed.

Variations

- This exercise can be done with both arms at once. In that case, you'll have to decrease the amount of weight you're using. You can also do bent-over rows with a barbell. The body mechanics change, with these variations. You'll be standing with your knees bent, body bent forward at the waist, your abs tight. If you're using a barbell, pull the bar up to your chest, as shown below.
- T-Bar rows are another option. This exercise, done on a piece of gym apparatus designed for that one exercise, matches the body mechanics of barbell rowing.

Upright Rows

Standard upright rows work the upper and middle back and some shoulder muscles.

Starting Position Stand with your knees slightly flexed, shoulder-width apart, back straight, pelvis tucked. Hold the barbell in front of your thighs, hands close together, palms facing you.

Movement

A. Exhale as you pull the bar up along the front of your body, leading with your elbows, until your upper arms are at a level about parallel with your shoulders.

B. Inhale and slowly return to the starting position.

Notes

- Keep your chin level.
- Don't arch your back.
- Keep your shoulders dropped.
- Your elbows should be drawn up no higher than your shoulders. (Slightly higher, an inch or so, may be safe for some people.)

CAUTION: This may be a risky exercise if you have elbow tendinitis, shoulder problems, or tightness in the neck.

Pull-Up (Chin-Up)

(works lats, upper back, shoulder girdle, and rear deltoids)

Starting Position Place a bench under the bar. Stand on the bench and take hold of the bar in a wide enough grip so that when you're pulling yourself up, your forearms are perpendicular to the floor. Your palms are facing away from your body.

Movement

A. Lift off the bench, exhale, and pull your body up (with the bar in front of your body) until your chin is even with the bar.

B. Inhale and slowly lower your body until your elbows form approximately a 130–140-degree angle.

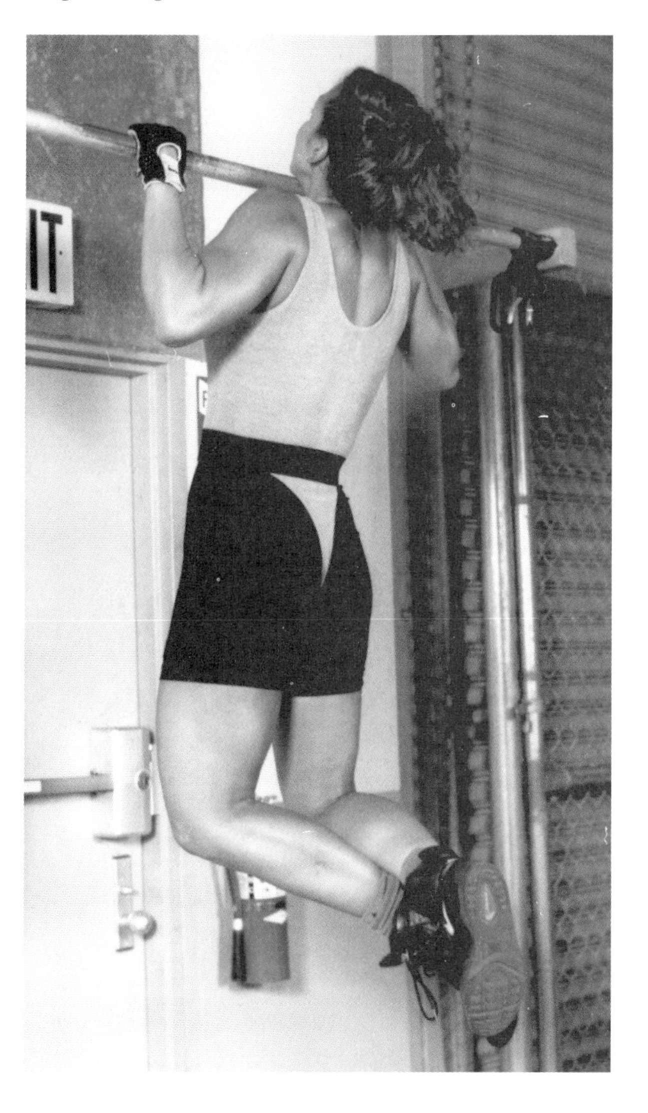

Notes

- Don't lower body all the way down.
- Keep the bar in front of your body for all pull-ups.

Variations

- If you're not strong enough to complete a pull-up with your legs hanging, keep your toes on the bench throughout the exercise.
- Do a pull-up as above, but reverse your hand grip—palms facing toward your body.
- Vary the width of your grips. A wide grip will focus on the outer back; a close grip will work the inner-back muscles more.

CAUTION: Use wrist straps if your wrists hurt during this exercise.

Dead Lift – Straight Leg

(works lower back, buttocks, and back of thighs)

Starting Position Grasp the bar in an overhand position, hands shoulder-width apart, and stand up so you are holding the bar in front of you. Your feet are positioned hip-width apart, knees slightly flexed. The abs should be tight and the pelvis neutral. Keep your back straight and your chin level.

CAUTION: This exercise is very valuable for strengthening the lower back, but it can cause injury to that region if performed with too much weight. Start with a very light weight (or even none at all) and work your way up gradually. If you've had low-back problems in the past, consult your orthopedist before doing this one. Regardless of your history, don't push yourself on this exercise. Do it near the start of your workout, before you tire yourself out with other exercises, and give it your full concentration. It also helps to do this exercise (or bent-knee dead lifts) regularly. If you feel *any* discomfort, stop immediately.

Movement

A. Keeping your back flat and your legs almost straight, inhale as you bend over at the waist and lower the bar as close to the floor as you can without bending your knees or rounding your back. You must be able to lower the bar to at least below your knees in order for this exercise to be safe.

B. Exhale, keeping your back completely flat, as you lift your body up to an erect position. The bar should practically drag along the front of your legs.

Variation This exercise can be performed with dumbbells. The movement mechanics are the same.

Notes

- Don't lean over backwards or bend your elbows as you lift your body up.
- Keep the bar or dumbbells close to your legs.
- Don't lock your knees and don't fully bend them; keep them slightly flexed throughout the exercise.
- Strive for controlled and even movements.

Dead Lift – Bent Knee

(works lower back, buttocks, and back of thighs)

Although this exercise is very valuable for strengthening the lower back, it can cause injury to that region if performed with too much weight (see Caution box below). Start with a very light weight (or even none at all) and work your way up gradually. If you've had low-back problems in the past, consult your orthopedist before doing this one. Regardless of your history, don't push yourself on this exercise. Do it near the start of your workout, before you tire yourself out with other exercises, and give it your full concentration. It also helps to do this exercise (or straight-leg dead lifts) regularly. If you feel any discomfort, stop immediately.

Starting Position Stand with your feet hip-width apart. Drop your buttocks so your thighs are roughly parallel to the floor. Grab the bar in an overhand position, hands shoulder-width apart, and lift the bar up slightly so as to position it over your feet.

Movement

A. Exhale as you slowly pull the bar up along the front of your legs while straightening your body.

B. Inhale and slowly reverse the movement. Keep your head up and keep your knees open (don't let them buckle inward).

Notes

- Keep your arms straight throughout the exercise.
- Keep the bar or dumbbells close to your body throughout the exercise.
- Don't lean back when you come up to the standing position.

Variation This exercise can be performed with dumbbells. The movement mechanics are the same.

> CAUTION: Anyone with a weak lower back or any kind of lower-back problem should approach this exercise with extreme caution. If you do it at all, start with a very light weight and add resistance gradually as your back becomes stronger.

Back Extension on Roman Chair

(works lower-back muscles)

Starting Position Position yourself face-down on the Roman chair. Your hands can be across your chest or resting on your lower back. The neck is straight.

Movement

A. Inhale as you lower your body about one quarter of the way toward the floor.

B. Exhale as you lift your body up parallel to the floor, no higher.

Notes

- Strive for controlled and even movements.
- Lower your torso only one quarter of the way toward the floor.
- Don't lift up any higher than parallel to the floor.
- Keep your neck straight.

CAUTION: Avoid this exercise if you have lower-back problems.

Specific Stretches for Back Muscles

Back Stretch 1

Turn your palm(s) outward and hang from an upright pole or door frame, either with both hands at once or one at a time. Hold and breathe for 20 seconds.

Back Stretch 2

Interlace your hands (palms toward you), and push your arms away from your body as you round your back and drop your chin. Hold and breathe for 20 seconds.

Shoulders

The shoulders are one of the most vulnerable and easily injured areas of your body—that is, if you don't train them correctly.

It seems that more people injure their shoulders in the gym than any other muscle/joint combination. There are two ways these injuries happen. Over the long run, people may train their shoulders using unsafe range of motion. Alternatively, people injure their shoulders in one set (or one rep) of an exercise, by overloading the deltoid muscles while also using unsafe range of motion in the shoulder joint.

The solution is to use controlled movements when training the shoulders. This is true for all exercises, but it's especially important when training the shoulders or when the deltoids are actively involved in an exercise. We have to be extra cautious because of the complexity of the shoulder joint. The shoulder is basically designed for mobility; therefore, the deltoid muscles should be developed with their function and ability to move in mind.

Pay close attention to the directions given for each individual shoulder exercise below. Preventing shoulder injury is always a key factor in these instructions. If some movements seem odd or unnatural, that's probably because you learned to exercise in a less safe way.

Protecting the shoulders from injury is paramount to long-term exercise adherence. If you develop shoulder impingement (from overuse, using an unsafe range of motion) or in any way injure the shoulder joint, you may be unable to train your upper body for weeks, possibly even months, at a time

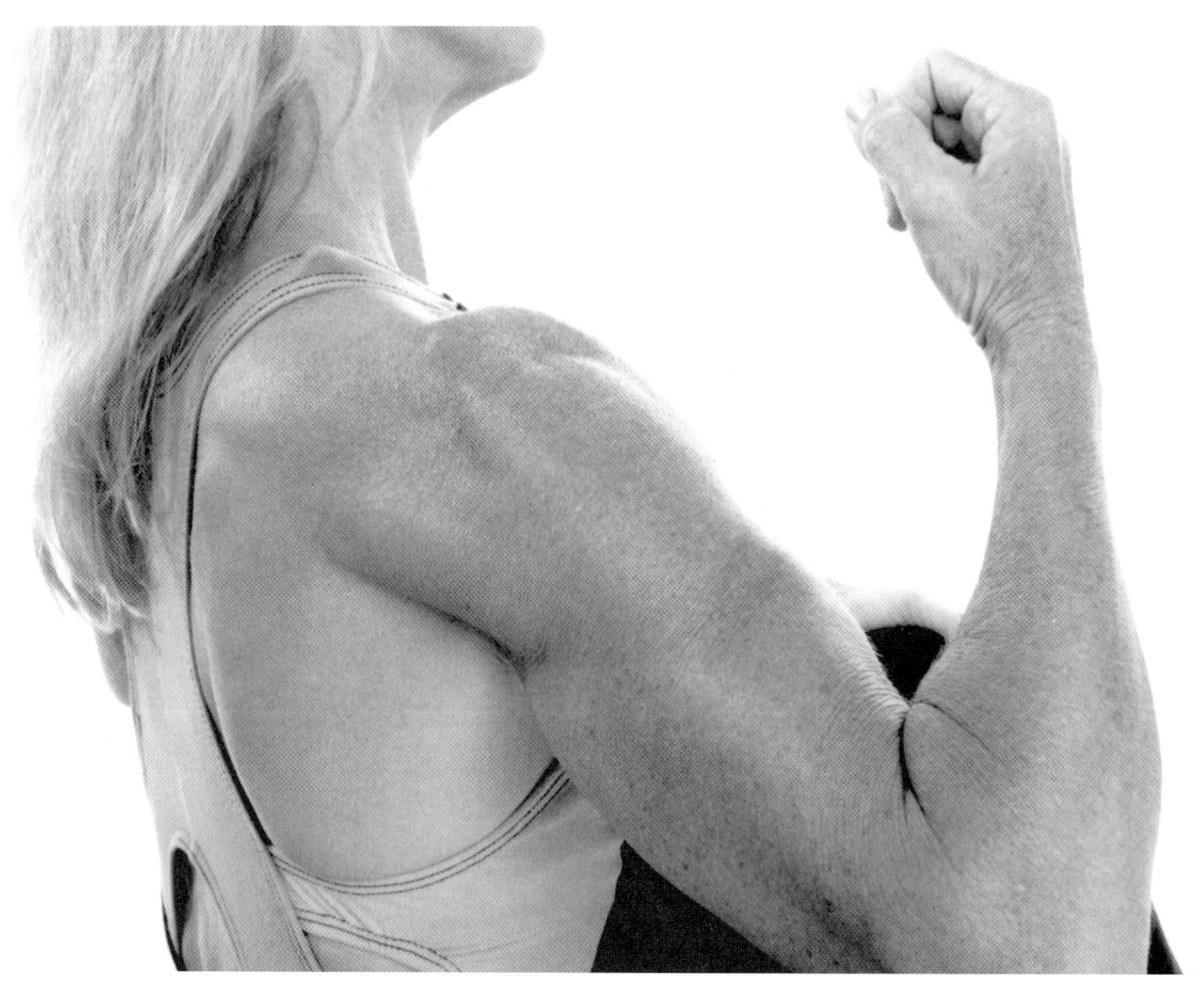

Shoulder Press

(works top of shoulder)

Starting Position Sit on a bench. If you don't have a strong back, use a bench with a back support. Hold the dumbbells so they are about level with your mouth, palms facing forward. Beginners, turn the palms toward your head.

Movement

A. Exhale as you press the dumbbells straight up, being careful not to fully extend your elbows. This will keep the stress off the elbows and on the deltoid muscles, where it's supposed to be.

B. Inhale as you slowly lower the weights to the starting position.

Notes

- Keep feet flat on the floor (to stabilize the back).
- Strive for controlled and even movements.
- Don't fully extend the arms as you press up.
- Press the dumbbells straight up. Don't bring them together overhead. If you do so, you're placing unnecessary strain on the shoulder joint without further benefit to the muscle.

Variations

- For beginners, you can do dumbbell presses with your palms facing in toward your head.
- You can alternate arms instead of doing both at once.
- You can perform a shoulder press with one arm while leaning on your side on an incline bench, as shown.

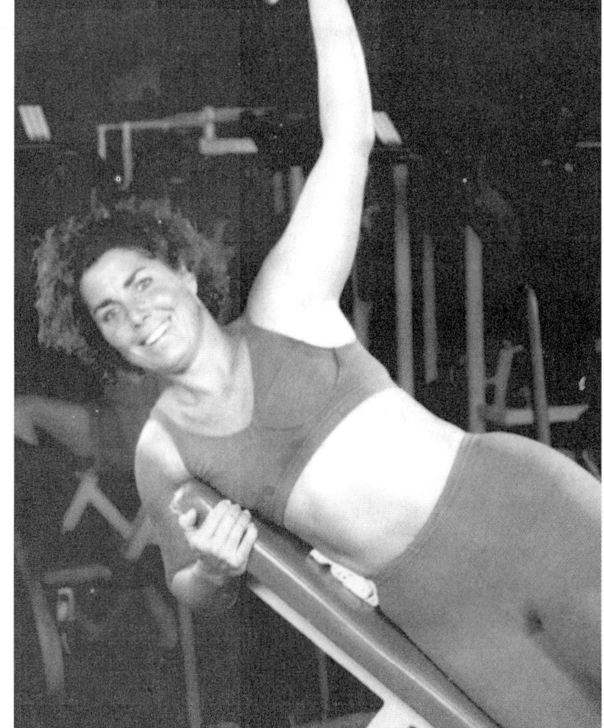

- *Bar Press* This exercise can be performed using a bar. The starting position and movements are the same as for a dumbbell press, only it's the bar that is level with the mouth. The hands should grasp the bar far enough apart so that your forearms form right angles with the bar (i.e., forearms perpendicular to the floor). You can press either to the front or to the back of your neck. Beginners, press to the front.

CAUTION: If you have shoulder problems, you may not be able to do press exercises.

Lateral Raise

(works outer shoulder)

Starting Position Stand with your legs hip-width apart. Let your spine remain neutral (allow its natural curve). Keep your chin level. Do not bend forward at the waist. Keep the abdominals tight. Hold a dumbbell in each hand, arms hanging down beside you.

Movement

A. Exhale as you lift the dumbbells straight out to your sides to about shoulder height.

B. Inhale as you slowly lower the dumbbells to starting position.

Notes

- Keep wrists straight.
- Strive for controlled and even movements.
- Don't lean forward at the waist.
- Keep the hips stable; don't rock back and forth.
- Don't bring your arms above your shoulders. If you do, you're placing unnecessary stress on the shoulder joint without further benefit to the muscle.

Variations

- *One-Arm Lateral Raise* The movement is the same, only you're lifting one arm at a time. You can complete an entire set with one arm, then switch to the other, or you can alternate arms within the set. Be careful not to lean to the side when working with one arm at a time.
- *Hanging One-Arm Lateral Raise* Hang from any stationary object by grabbing the object with one hand, placing your feet near the base of it, and leaning away from it as far as you can. Lift the dumbbell as shown.

CAUTION: Shoulder problems will prevent you from doing lateral raises.

Front Shoulder Raise

(works front of shoulders)

Starting Position Stand with the dumbbells held in front of your thighs, arms straight, elbows slightly bent, palms facing thighs, knees relaxed, pelvis and spine neutral.

Movement

A. Exhale as you raise your arm to shoulder level, no higher.

B. Inhale as you slowly lower the weight back to the starting position.

Notes

- Keep wrist straight.
- Strive for controlled and even movements.
- Don't arch your back.
- Don't swing your body back and forth. Keep your trunk motionless.
- Don't lift arm higher than shoulder level.

Variations

- *Alternate-Arm Raise* You'll probably have to do this anyway when you graduate to more intense training workloads. Alternate reps, not sets—that is, do left, right, left, right, etc.—until you've completed the prescribed number of reps with each arm.
- *Half-Prone Front Shoulder Raise* Palms face each other; otherwise follow directions above.
- *Front Shoulder Raises with Internal Shoulder Rotation* Perform as you would a standard front shoulder raise but, as you're lifting your arms up, gradually twist them (movement originates at the shoulders) so your thumbs are nearly turned toward the floor at the top of the movement. Don't twist farther or faster than what feels comfortable.
- *Front Shoulder Raises with Palms Turned Out* The palms are turned out (facing up as you lift and away from the thighs); otherwise follow directions for standard front shoulder raises.
- *Front Shoulder Raises with Olympic Plate* Same as standard front shoulder raise, only instead of holding dumbbells, you are holding a single Olympic plate between your hands (hold it with one hand on each side of the outer rim).

CAUTION: If you have shoulder problems, you may not be able to do this exercise.

Rear Delt Raise

(works back of shoulders)

Starting Position Lie prone (facedown) on an incline bench that is positioned at about a 30-degree angle. Hold a dumbbell in each hand, arms hanging straight down, elbows slightly bent. Your neck should remain neutral.

Movement

A. Exhale as you raise the dumbbells out to your sides, to shoulder height only.

B. Inhale as you slowly lower the dumbbells to starting position.

Notes

- Strive for controlled and even movements.
- Arms go no higher than shoulder height.
- Keep wrists straight.
- Keep neck straight.
- Keep elbows only slightly bent (relaxed), not fully bent.

CAUTION: If you have shoulder problems, you may not be able to do this exercise.

Variations

- *Standing Rear Delt Raise* This is an advanced way to perform the exercise, because your abdominal and erector muscles are stabilizing the trunk of your body. While performing the exercise, you lean forward at the waist at approximately a 30-degree angle. The movement is the same as on an incline bench.
- *Seated Rear Delt Raise* As shown below, sit on the end of a stable bench, feet placed on an elevated surface. Lean forward and rest your chest on the tops of your thighs, then follow the directions for the incline rear delt raise.

Arnold Press

(works top and front of shoulder)

Starting Position Sit on a bench with a back support. Place your feet flat on the floor. Hold the dumbbells in front of you, close to your body. They'll be level with your mouth, palms facing toward you.

Movement

A. Exhale as you press both dumbbells up to arm's length, gradually turning them as you go, so that at the top of the movement your palms are facing away from you. Don't lock the elbows.

B. Slowly lower the weights to starting position, gradually turning your palms back in as you do.

Notes

- Strive for controlled and even movements.
- Don't fully extend your arms.
- Don't bring the weights together overhead.
- Keep your feet flat on the floor.

CAUTION: If you have shoulder problems, you may not be able to do this exercise.

Specific Stretches for the Shoulders

Shoulder Stretch 1

Standing, take hold of your left forearm and pull your arm across the front of your body as far as you can, making sure your left shoulder doesn't roll forward. Hold and breathe for 20 seconds. Repeat on other side.

NOTE: Also works to stretch the chest muscles.

Shoulder Stretch 2

Holding your elbow at a right angle, fingers pointed up, place your forearm against a flat surface, then gently twist your torso out away from the lifted arm. Hold and breathe for 20 seconds; repeat with other arm.

Biceps

Most people find biceps the easiest muscle in the body to train, probably because bicep exercises match common everyday movements. Each time you pick up a bag of groceries, you're essentially doing a bicep curl. Consequently, out of all the upper-body muscles, biceps are the muscles that are usually the least atrophied in sedentary people.

Biceps are also fun to train. During a workout, your biceps are always in full view, thus you're able to instantly see what you're doing right or wrong, and make corrections accordingly. Bicep exercises don't require as much knowledge of body mechanics as other exercises (e.g., squats). That, of course, makes them much easier to perform.

Bicep development brought on by everyday activities can eventually increase the likelihood of elbow problems. That's because the other muscle in the upper arm, the tricep, is not built as up as much by everyday movements. In order for the triceps to contract (work) you have to straighten out your elbow against resistance, which is not a move we often make in everyday life. If you're training your biceps with weights, this imbalance can be amplified, and it's especially important to include a tricep workout in your program too.

The concept of "following the carrying angle" applies to bicep exercises in particular. It means that at the beginning and end of each repetition the shoulder, elbow, and wrist are in a plumb line to the floor. Following the carrying angle will maximize the effort (and the benefit) of each repetition.

All the bicep exercises in this book involve only one movement, with the exception of one hammer curl variation. You'll start and finish each exercise either with the palms facing up (forward), or with the palms in a half-prone position, facing in toward the body. Exercises done in the half-prone position emphasize the top of the bicep and are a valuable part of your program. However, less muscle is involved in half-prone exercises, so combining the two positions in one exercise may compromise results. Do one exercise at a time and don't rotate your hands while performing the exercise, except when performing hammer curls.

Standard Barbell Curl

(works front of upper arm)

Starting Position Stand with your knees relaxed, pelvis tucked, shoulders dropped, chin level, feet approximately shoulder-width apart. Hold the barbell in front of you, palms facing forward, arms extended straight down from the shoulders.

Movement

A. Exhale as you flex (bend) your elbows, bringing the barbell about three-quarters of the way up toward your shoulders.

B. Inhale as you return to the starting position.

Notes

- Keep your wrists straight.
- Don't swing the weights; strive for controlled and even movements.
- For maximum benefit, stop about three-quarters of the way up, at the "peak contraction."
- Don't rock your body or lean backward.
- Keep your elbows close to your body.
- Don't lock your elbows at the bottom of the movement.

CAUTION: Sometimes when people do barbell curls, they feel a burning on the inside of their arms, right at the elbow. If you are experiencing pain at the elbow, do all your curls with dumbbells (not barbells), and rotate the arms into a half-prone position (palms facing in toward the body) for the downward phase of each rep. This rotation may reduce the training benefit slightly, so it should only be done by those who experience elbow trouble.

Variations

- Try doing curls with dumbbells too. The body mechanics are exactly the same as with a barbell. You can lift both dumbbells at once, but you'll probably be able to lift heavier weights if you alternate your arms. Do one rep with the left arm, then one with the right arm, etc., until you've done enough reps with each arm—the total number of movements will thus be double the usual.
- You can also do barbell curls with the EZ Curl Bar (zigzag shape). This bar is recommended if you have weak wrists.

Hammer Curl

(works front of upper arm)

Starting Position Stand with your knees relaxed, pelvis tucked, shoulders dropped, chin level, and feet approximately shoulder-width apart. Hold a dumbbell in each hand with your palms turned in toward your body.

Movement

A. Exhale and flex (bend) your elbows as you bring the dumbbells about ¾ of the way up toward your shoulders.

B. Inhale as you return to the starting position.

Notes

- Keep the wrists straight.
- Don't swing the weights; strive for controlled and even movements.
- Stop about ¾ of the way up (at "peak contraction") for maximum benefit.
- Don't rock your body or lean backward.
- Keep your elbows close to your body.
- Don't lock your elbows at the bottom of the movement.

Variations

- Alternate arms—one rep with the left arm, then one with the right arm, etc.; the total number of reps will be twice the usual number.
- *Seated Hammer Curl* The body mechanics are the same, but the dumbbells are suspended at your sides. Seated hammer curls are harder to perform.
- *Advanced Hammer Curl* Start as in a standard hammer curl, but as you curl you arm up toward your shoulder, rotate your elbow until your palm is facing up.

> CAUTION: If you have elbow tendinitis, you may not be able to perform hammer curls.

Preacher Curl

(works front of upper arm)

Starting Position Sit on the preacher bench with both arms hanging over the top of the arm pad. Hold your hands shoulder-width apart. Your elbows should be slightly bent.

If you have weak wrists, use the EZ Curl Bar. Otherwise, the straight bar is preferable, because using a straight bar increases the contraction of the biceps.

Movement

A. Exhale and bend your elbows as you bring the bar up, until your forearms are perpendicular to the floor.

B. Inhale as you return to the starting position. Be careful to keep your elbows slightly bent.

Notes

- Keep your wrists straight.
- Keep elbows bent at the bottom of the movement.
- Strive to use slow, controlled movements.
- Keep arms parallel to each other on the preacher pad.
- Stop when forearms are perpendicular to the floor (at peak contraction), for maximum benefit.

Variations

- Preacher curls can be performed with dumbbells too—the movement is exactly the same.
- *One-Arm Preacher Curl* (with dumbbell) Done in the same manner, but hang just one arm over the preacher pad at a time. Alternate sets—a full set with the right arm, then a full set with the left arm, etc.
- Hammer curls can also be done on a preacher bench. Keep your palms turned in (facing to the side) throughout the exercise, unless performing the advanced variation.

CAUTION: If you have elbow tendinitis, you may not be able to perform either barbell or dumbbell curls.

Concentration Curl
(works front of upper arm)

Starting Position Sit on the edge of a bench, both feet planted firmly on the floor, knees open wide. With your right hand, hold a dumbbell between your legs at arm's length, with the back of the upper right arm resting against the inner right thigh, near the knee. You will be leaning slightly forward.

CAUTION: If you have elbow tendinitis, you may not be able to perform this exercise.

Movement

A. Exhale and curl the dumbbell up by bending your elbow, until the dumbbell is ¾ of the way to your shoulder.

B. Inhale as you slowly lower the weight to the starting position.

Notes

- Don't bend the wrists.
- Keep the upper portion of the working arm vertical.

Variation Perform concentration curls holding the dumbbell in a hammer curl position. Advanced exercisers may use the rotating position described in the hammer curl variation on page 82.

High-Pulley Cable Curl

(works front of upper arms)

Starting Position Grasp a cable handle in each hand, palms facing up. Center yourself in between the two pulleys. Lift both arms until they're even with your shoulders. Drop your shoulder blades. Have your elbows slightly bent. Stand with a straight back. Knees are dropped slightly.

Movement

A. Exhale and bend your elbows, bringing the handles about ¾ of the way in and down toward your shoulders.

B. Inhale and slowly return to the starting position.

Notes

- Keep your wrists straight.
- Keep the shoulder blades dropped.
- Stop at ¾ of the way in, at peak contraction, for maximum benefit.
- Don't lean forward at the waist.
- Strive for controlled and even movements.

CAUTION: If you have elbow tendinitis, you may not be able to perform this exercise.

Low-Pulley Cable Curl

(works front of upper arm)

Starting Position Hold the cable bar in both hands. Extend your arms straight down from your shoulders. The elbows are slightly bent, the back is straight, knees are dropped slightly.

Caution: If you have elbow tendinitis, you may not be able to perform this exercise.

Movement

A. Exhale as you bend your elbows, bringing the bar about three-quarters of the way up toward your shoulders.

B. Inhale and slowly lower the bar back to the starting position.

Notes

- Keep wrists straight.
- Don't lean backwards.
- Strive for controlled and even movements.
- Stop three-quarters of the way up, at peak contraction, for maximum benefit.

Specific Stretch for Biceps

Lift and extend both arms straight out beside you. Turn thumbs down and gently pull arms back.

The most important thing to keep in mind when performing tricep exercises is not to lock the elbows. The safest grip when doing tricep work with dumbbells is a half-prone position with the palms faced in toward the body. This position also presents a mechanical advantage which may lead to quicker muscle development.

Black-Eye (French Press)

(works back of upper arm)

Starting Position Lie back on a flat bench, feet flat on floor or bench. Beginners, hold a dumbbell in your right hand (not shown) with your arm extended toward the ceiling. Use your left hand to support your upper right arm, near the elbow. Do not lock the right elbow.

Movement

A. Inhale as you slowly lower the dumbbell to your shoulder, keeping the elbow pointed toward the ceiling.

B. Exhale as you lift the dumbbell back up to the starting position.

C. Perform one complete set, then switch hands and repeat.

Notes

- Strive for controlled and even movements.
- Don't lock elbow as you lift up the dumbbell.
- Don't allow the working arm to move; keep the elbow pointed toward the ceiling.

Variations

- Done with both arms at once as shown at left—a more advanced version—you give up the support of the other arm.
- Perform the exercise using a barbell (see below). Hold the bar with your hands shoulder-width apart. Lower the bar to just above your forehead.

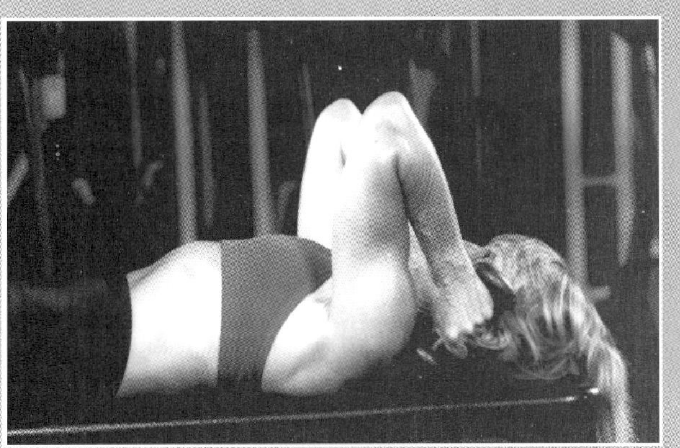

Overhead Extension

(works back of upper arm)

Starting Position Sit on a bench with a back support. Hold a single dumbbell with both hands in a vertical position over your head, palms up and thumbs wrapped around the handle. Keep upper arms close to your head, elbows pointing toward the ceiling. Extend your arms, but be sure not to lock your elbows.

Movement

A. Inhale as you bend your arms at the elbows, so that the dumbbell is slowly lowered behind your neck.

B. Exhale as you straighten your arms and lift the dumbbell back up to the starting position.

Notes

- Keep your back straight.
- Strive for controlled and even movements.
- Don't bounce the dumbbell off your traps as you lower the weight.

Variation *One-Arm Overhead Extension* Grip a dumbbell in the normal fashion (by the handle), with one hand only. Point the elbow toward the ceiling, arm close to head. Use the other hand to support the working arm, as with the previous, Black-Eye, exercise. Movement is the same as above; then repeat with other arm.

Reverse-Grip Bench Press

(works back of upper arm)

Starting Position Lie flat on a bench press rack. Position your body as you would if you were doing a bench press. Grip the bar as if you were doing a bicep curl, palms facing up. Your grip should be just as wide as your rib cage.

Movement

A. Inhale as you lower the bar down toward your lower rib cage.

B. Exhale as you press the bar back up to the starting position.

Notes

- Don't lock your elbows at the top of the press.
- Don't let the bar touch your body as you lower it.
- Strive for controlled and even movements.
- Keep your wrists straight throughout the entire exercise.

Kickback

(works back of upper arm)

Starting Position Lean forward, supporting your weight by resting your right hand on a bench; do not lock the right elbow. Make sure your back and neck are straight, abs contracted. Hold a dumbbell in your left hand, then lift the upper arm so it's parallel to the floor. Elbow is bent so the weight is just below the shoulder.

Movement

A. Exhale as you press the dumbbell back until the entire arm is parallel to the floor.

B. Inhale as you return the weight to the starting position.

Notes

- Keep the working elbow lifted and close to your body.
- Strive for controlled and even movements.
- Keep the elbow of your supporting arm slightly bent.

Straight-Arm Kickback

(works top portion of back of upper arm)

Starting Position Stand with a bench at your side and lean forward, resting one hand on the bench and holding a dumbbell in the other hand. Neither elbow is locked. Keep the back straight. The arm holding the dumbbell is extended down toward the floor.

Movement

A. Exhale as you raise the dumbbell up until your entire arm is parallel to the floor. Don't bend your elbow; the lifting arm should remain straight.

B. Inhale as you return to starting position.

Note Strive for controlled and even movements; don't swing the dumbbell.

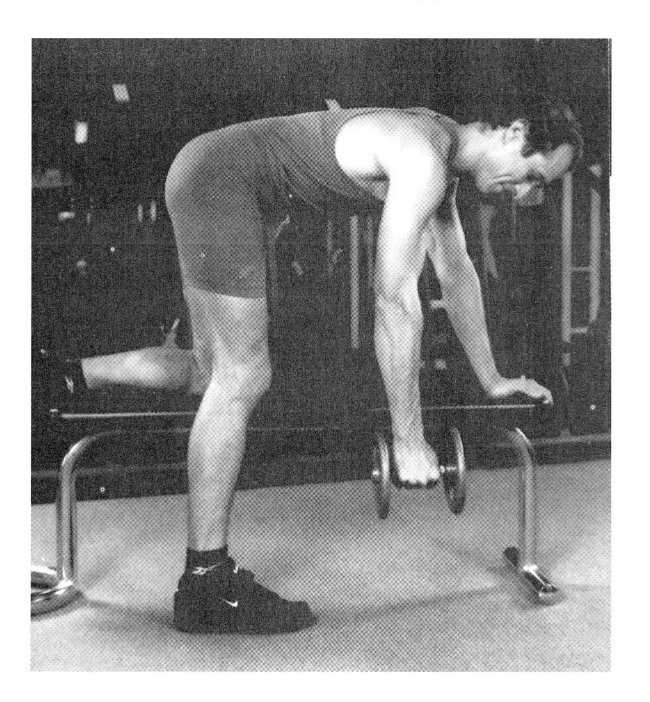

RECOMMENDED: This exercise is recommended for anyone with elbow tendinitis, because there is no movement at the elbows.

Combination Kickback

(works entire back of upper arm)

This exercise combines the two on this spread: *Kickback* and *Straight-Arm Kickback*.

Starting Position Stand with a bench at your side and lean forward, resting one hand on the bench and holding a dumbbell in the other hand. Neither elbow is locked. Keep the back straight. The arm holding the dumbbell is extended down toward the floor.

Movement

A. Exhale as you raise the dumbbell up until your entire arm is parallel to the floor. Don't bend your elbow; the lifting arm should remain straight.

B. Now bend your elbow and lower the weight to just below the shoulder, while keeping the upper arm parallel to the floor.

C. Exhale as you press the dumbbell back until your entire arm is again parallel to the floor.

D. Inhale as you lower the entire straight arm down to starting position. These four movements together constitute one rep.

Note Strive for controlled and even movements; don't swing the dumbbell.

Straight-Arm Cable Press

(works top portion of back of upper arm)

Starting Position Stand in front of a bar used for lat pulls, with your arms fully extended at shoulder level. Grip the bar with your palms facing downward.

Movement

A. Exhale as you press the bar down toward your legs.

B. Inhale as you slowly allow the bar to return to the starting position. Don't allow the bar to go any higher than shoulder level.

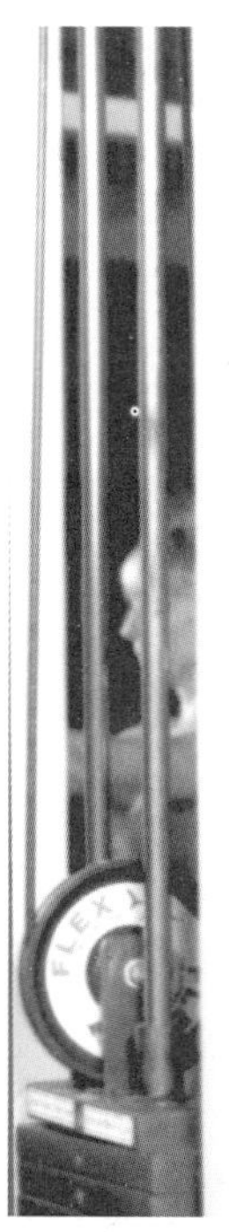

Notes

- Keep the elbows straight, but not locked, throughout the entire exercise.
- Strive for controlled, even movements.
- This exercise is recommended for anyone with elbow tendinitis because there is no movement at the elbows.

Cable Rope Pull

(works outer portion of back of upper arms)

Starting Position Stand in front of the rope. Grip the rope ends with your palms facing down toward the floor. Elbows are by the sides of your body.

Movement

A. Exhale as you press the rope down by straightening out your arms, spreading your hands as you do so. Don't lock your elbows.

B. Inhale as you allow the rope to return to the starting position. Keep your elbows by your sides throughout the exercise.

Notes

- Strive for controlled and even movements.
- Don't allow your elbows to lift; keep them by your sides.
- Don't lock your elbows during the rope press.

Variation This exercise can also be done with the curved (W-shaped) bar.

Specific Stretch for Triceps

Lift right arm overhead with the elbow bent. Gently push back on the right elbow with the left hand. Hold and breathe for 20 seconds. Repeat with other arm.

Calf Muscles

Calf training is an integral, but often omitted, part of any workout regimen. It's important to keep the calf muscles strong because these muscles help stabilize the ankles and knees. If you have strong calf muscles you'll be less likely to develop knee and ankle problems and you'll be at less risk for ankle and knee injury. From the point of view of body shaping, your calves are also one of the most visible parts of your body if you ever wear shorts, dresses, or skirts!

Each time you exercise your calf muscles, be sure to press your heels down as far as possible and lift your heels up as high as you can (the whole time keeping the balls of your feet on the foot pad). By doing this, you're making sure the entire length of the muscle is being worked. Also keep your back straight when performing standing calf raises, and never bend your knees when doing calf exercises of any kind.

Contrary to popular belief, it's not necessary to turn your feet in or out in order to target specific areas of the calf muscles. These turned positions place a lot of stress on the knees unless you also externally rotate the hips out as you turn your feet out, and internally rotate the hips in as you turn your feet in. A safer, easier way to target specific parts of the calf is to keep your feet pointing straight ahead and either transfer the greater part of your weight to the inside of each foot, focusing on the area around the big toe (this replaces the turned-in position and emphasizes the inner calf), or transfer the greater part of your weight to the outside of each foot, focusing on the area around the baby toe (this replaces the turned-out position and emphasizes the outer calf). If you want to focus on the center of the big calf muscle (gastrocnemius), distribute the weight evenly across the ball of each foot.

No matter which way you are doing it, the balls of the feet always remain flat on the foot pad; some of the weight is merely transferred from side to side (or distributed evenly). Also, the ankles are never tilted in or out; they remain straight throughout the entire exercise, no matter where the focus is placed.

Standing Calf Raise

(works back of lower leg)

Starting Position Follow the directions on the gym equipment. Make sure the shoulder pads are high enough so you can perform your calf exercises with your knees and back straight. Distribute the weight on your feet in one of the three ways described above in the introductory part of this section.

Movement

A. Exhale as you lift your heels up as high as you're able.

B. Inhale as you slowly lower your heels down as far as you can.

Notes

- Keep the balls of your feet in place.
- Strive for controlled and even movements.
- Perform at least one set with each of the three weight distributions.
- Keep your back and knees straight throughout the exercise.
- Keep the hips stable; don't move them back and forth.

Variation *Standing Dumbbell Calf Raise* Stand with the ball of your right foot on an elevated surface. Wrap your left ankle around your right. Hold a dumbbell in your right hand, balance with your left hand. Perform the calf raises as described above. Then switch legs. Perform at least one set with each of the three weight distributions.

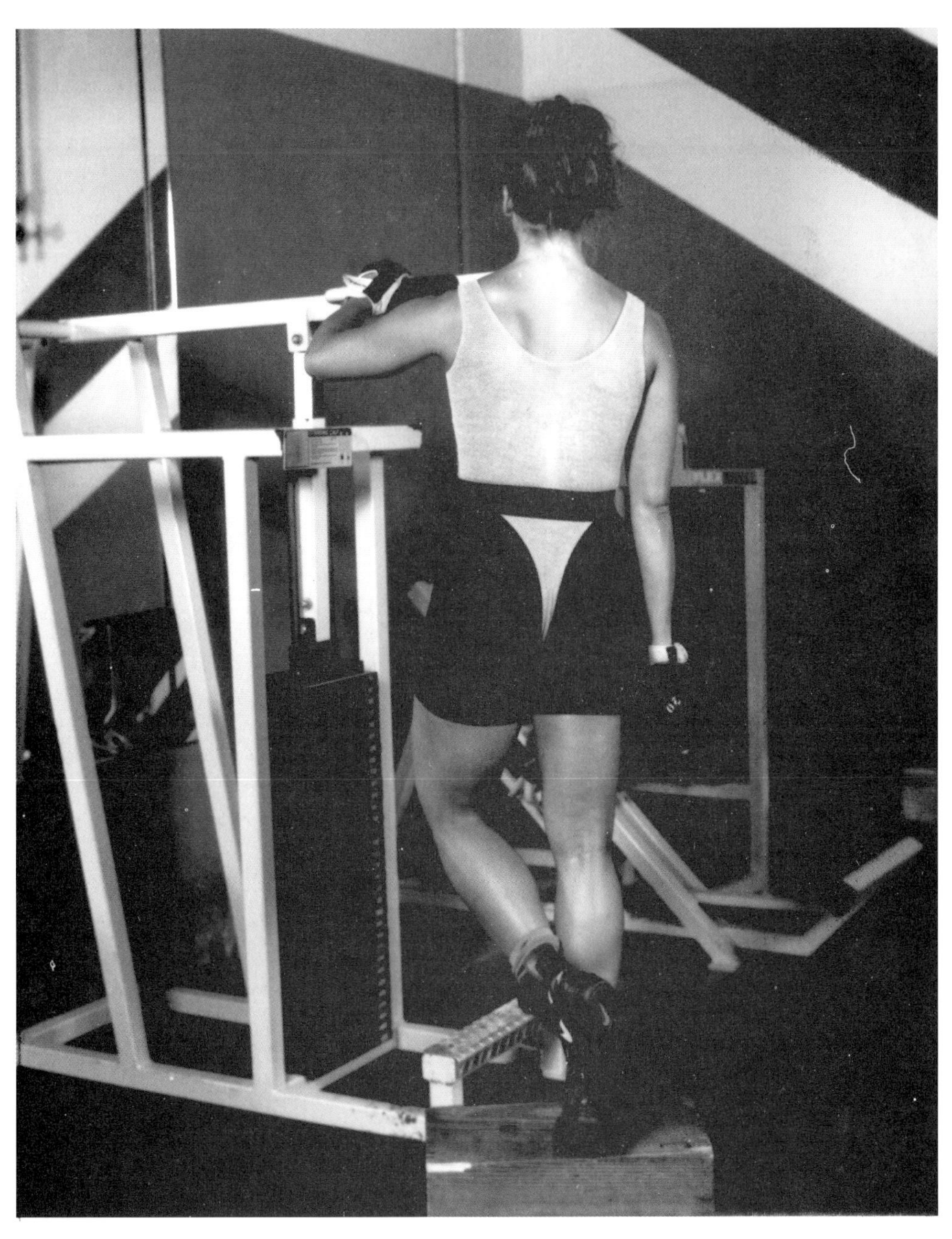

Seated Calf Raise

(works back of lower leg)

Starting Position Follow the directions on the gym equipment. Distribute the weight on your feet in one of the three ways described in the introductory part of this section.

Movement

A. Exhale as you lift your heels up as high as you're able.

B. Inhale as you slowly lower your heels down as far as you can.

Notes

- Keep the balls of your feet in place.
- Strive for controlled and even movements.
- Perform at least one set with each of the three weight distributions.

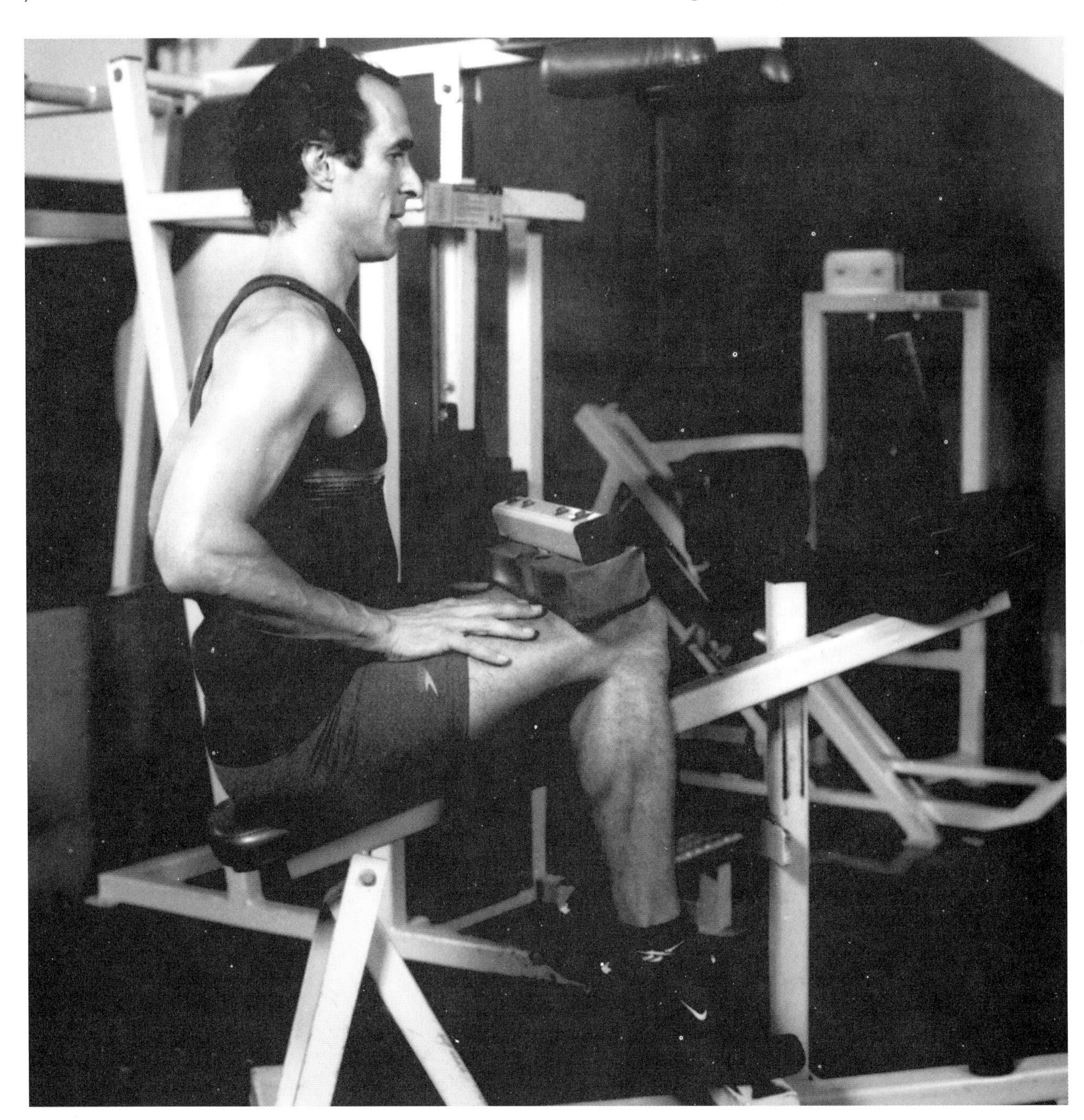

Variation *Seated Dumbbell Calf Raises* Sit on a bench with the dumbbells on top of your legs close to your knees. Place the balls of your feet on the edge of an elevated surface. Perform the calf raises as described above. Do at least one set with each of the three weight distributions.

Forearms and Wrists

Even though these exercises may seem unimportant, they're not. The wrists and forearms are often weak links in your body. If the forearm and wrist muscles aren't strong, this may inhibit your ability to work your larger muscle groups to full capacity. For example, weak forearms limit the amount of weight you can lift while doing lat (back) work, because they give out before the larger back muscles do.

Although the wrists and forearms must not be ignored, you needn't feel compelled to work them too often. Three or four sets a week should be enough to keep these muscles strong and in balance with the rest of your body.

Reverse Curl

(works forearms)

Starting Position Stand holding a set of dumbbells, or a barbell, in front of your thighs, palms facing toward your legs.

Movement

A. Exhale as you bend your elbows and lift up toward your shoulders, as shown.

B. Inhale and slowly return to starting position.

Notes

- Strive for controlled and even movements.
- Keep your wrists straight throughout the entire exercise.
- Keep your back straight.

Wrist Curls – Flexion

(works muscles of wrists)

Starting Position Hold a set of dumbbells or a barbell, and sit on a bench resting your forearms on your thighs so that your wrists are on top of your knees, palms facing up.

Movement

A. Exhale as you curl your wrists up as high as you can.

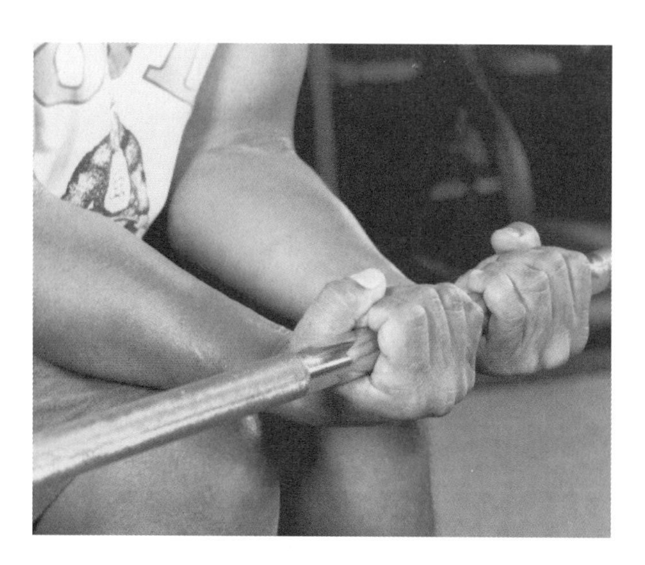

B. Inhale as you lower the weight so that the backs of your hands again touch the fronts of your knees, in starting position.

Extension

(works muscles of wrists)

Starting Position Hold a set of dumbbells, or a barbell, and sit on a bench resting your forearms on your thighs so that your wrists are on top of your knees, palms facing down.

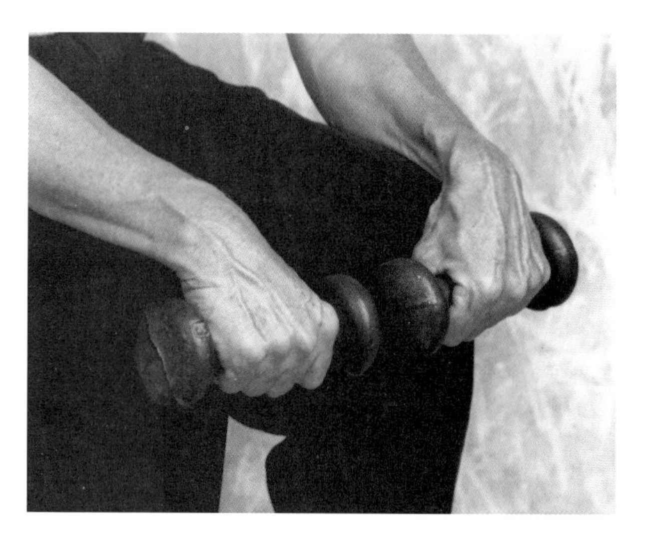

Movement

A. Exhale as you curl your wrists up as high as you can.

B. Inhale as you lower the weight so that the palms of your hands face down and your knuckles touch the front of your knees.

Abdominals

Appearances aside, abdominal exercises are probably the most important exercises for your physical health. When these muscles are strong, they take some of the workload off the lower back; strong "abs" help to support the lower back, stabilize your body, and protect your back from injury. Moreover, firm, developed abdominals help to hold the internal organs in place, which in turn also takes pressure off the lower-back area.

An effective abdominal program is crucial for maintaining erect posture and preventing low-back problems from occurring in the first place. Instead of doing 3 or 4 sets of 8–12 reps, as with most other exercises, we recommend you do fewer sets and work to muscle failure on each set. This method seems to be more effective at developing strong abdominal muscles.

For a beginner, failure may be just 3 reps. That's OK. As time goes on and as your abs become stronger, that number will increase. If, on the other hand, failure means doing 100 reps, it's time to increase the training stimulus. Abdominal muscles adapt to repeated training workloads, just as all muscle groups do.

Once your abs are conditioned, you should progressively perform the more advanced exercises. The abdominal exercises in this book are arranged into categories of beginning, intermediate, and advanced exercises. Also, always vary your ab exercises so as to use a variety of movements. That way, you'll be sure to target the entire abdominal plate, from a number of angles.

Contrary to popular myth and the advertising campaigns for some abdominal exercise gizmos, abdominal exercises will not help you lose the fat around your mid-section. Fat is shed fairly evenly all over your body—you can't "spot reduce." Aerobic exercise (and avoiding fatty foods) will help get rid of the fat. It's also helpful to practice pulling your stomach (abdominals) in and down, like squeezing them shut. Finally, here are two training tips that apply to all abdominal exercises:

- Always keep the knees bent when doing ab work, unless the legs are used in the performance of the exercise. Bent knees tilt the pelvis in such a way that there is less stress and strain on the lower-back (erector) muscles and more on the abdominal muscles, where it's supposed to be.
- Imagine that your abdominal area is like the bellows of an accordion. When you're lifting your body (away from gravity), always squeeze the bellows (abs) shut.

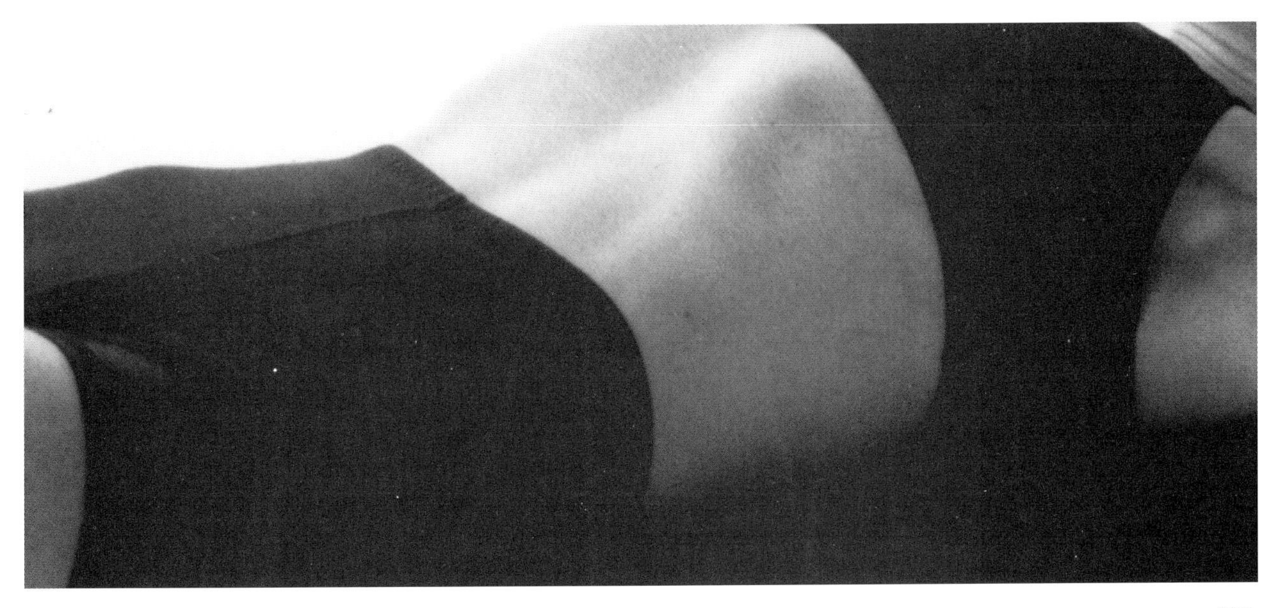

Tailbone Lift

(works abdominals)

This is an advanced abdominal exercise, with a variation for beginners.

Starting Position Lie on your back on a flat bench. If necessary, stabilize your upper body by holding on to a bench above your head. Extend your legs straight up toward the ceiling.

Movement

A. Exhale as you contract your abdominal muscles and lift your tailbone up off the bench.

B. Inhale as you slowly lower your tailbone back down.

Notes

- Don't lift your lower back off the bench, just your tailbone.
- Keep your legs perpendicular to the floor.
- Strive for controlled and even movements.
- Squeeze your abs shut like an accordion as you lift.

Variation Beginners, do this exercise with your knees bent, as shown below. Your thighs will still be pointing toward the ceiling.

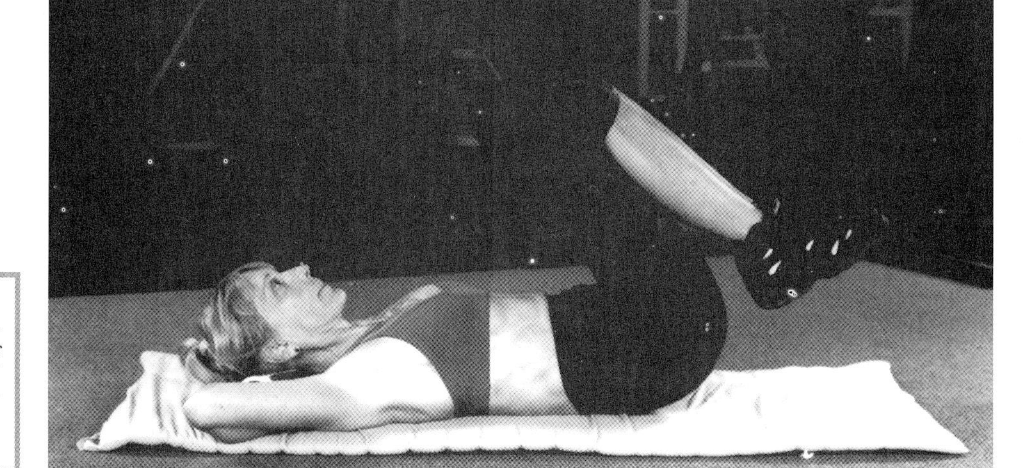

CAUTION: Avoid this exercise if you have lower-back problems.

Crunch

(works abdominals)

This is an advanced abdominal exercise, with a variation for beginners.

Starting Position Lie on your back. Extend your legs up toward the ceiling. Lift your upper body as high as you can. Shoulder blades should be off the floor. Extend your arms straight out in front of you, beside your hips, or place your fingertips behind your head for support (*don't* push on your head, though).

Movement

Press your upper body a little higher, then release, in short pulsing movements, exhaling each time you press up. Continue until you cannot do any more pulsing movements.

Variation If you are a beginner, do this exercise with your knees bent and your hands behind your head, as shown below.

Notes

- Keep your neck straight. Avoid the tendency to roll your head forward when you're pulsing up.
- Keep your abs squeezed shut throughout the exercise.

Curl-Up – Center

(works abdominals)

This is a beginning abdominal exercise, with variations for intermediate and advanced exercisers.

Starting Position Lie on your back, knees bent, feet flat on the floor. Place your hands behind your head, elbows pulled back.

Movement

A. Exhale as you slowly lift your shoulders and upper back off the floor as high as you can.
B. Inhale as you slowly lower them down.

Notes

- Keep your neck straight.
- Keep your elbows pulled back.
- Don't arch your back.
- Squeeze your abs shut as you lift.

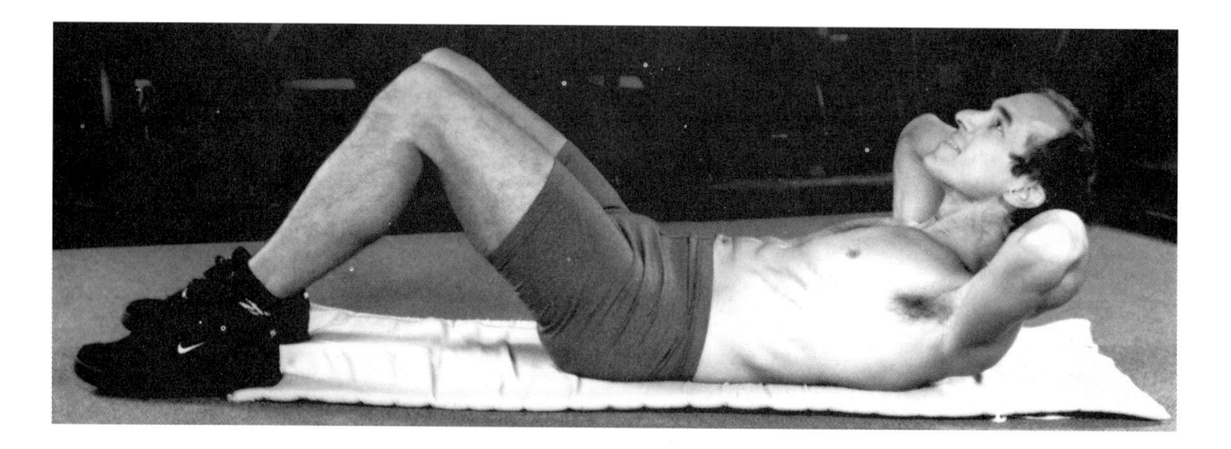

Variations

- If you're an intermediate, perform this exercise with your legs bent, feet off the floor, or legs straddled over a bench.
- If you are advanced, perform this exercise with your legs pointing straight up toward the ceiling, as shown here.

CAUTION: If you have elbow tendinitis, you may not be able to perform this exercise.

Side Curl-Up

(works abdominals and obliques)

This is an exercise designed for all levels of fitness. To increase the training stimulus, lift your body higher so the elbow comes closer to touching the knee.

Starting Position Lie on your back. Place your left hand behind your head, right hand on the floor. Place the back of your right ankle on top of your left knee.

Movement

A. Exhale as you lift your shoulders and upper back as high as you can, pressing the left elbow toward the right knee.

B. Inhale as you slowly lower back down.

C. Perform a full set, then reverse positions and repeat steps **A** and **B**.

Notes

- Strive for controlled and even movements.
- Don't arch your back.
- Squeeze abs shut as you lift.

Trunk Curl/Pelvic Tilt Combination

(works abdominals)

This is an intermediate to advanced abdominal exercise.

Starting Position Lie on your back, knees bent, feet flat on the floor. Place your hands behind your head.

Movement

A. Exhale and tilt your pelvis up at the same time that you slowly curl your upper back off the floor.

B. Inhale and slowly lower the entire body back down.

Notes

- Strive for controlled and even movements.
- Don't lift your lower back off the floor. Stop as soon as your hips are tilted up.
- Squeeze abs shut as you lift.

Knee-Up

(works hip flexors)

This is an advanced abdominal exercise with a super-advanced variation.

Starting Position Hang by your hands from a bar, with your thighs at a right angle to your chest.

Movement

A. Exhale as you slowly pull your knees up toward your chest, allowing your pelvis to roll upward.

B. Inhale and slowly lower your pelvis and legs back to the starting position.

Notes

- Don't allow your body to swing.
- Strive for controlled and even movements.

Variation Perform this exercise with your legs straight, or nearly straight, as you become more advanced.

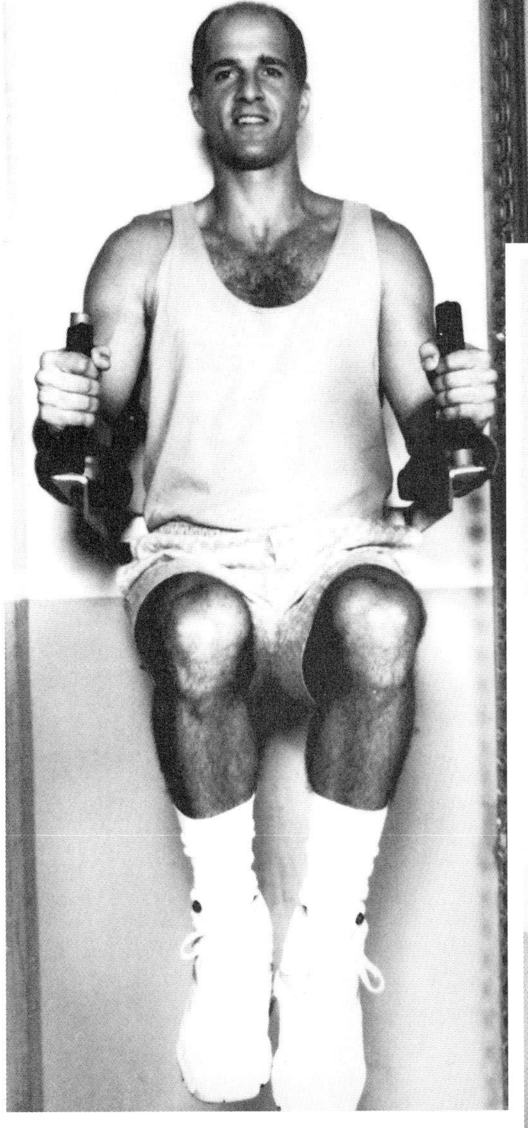

Bar Twist

(works waistline and lower-back muscles)

Bar twists are effective for all levels of fitness.

Starting Position Sit on the edge of a bench with a bar resting across your upper traps in back of your neck. The weight of the bar is dependent on your level of fitness and physical ability.

Movement Twist your entire upper body from side to side. Breathe normally.

Notes

- Twist as far as you can.
- Allow your head to turn naturally along with your torso; all movement originates at the waistline. Avoid the tendency to lead with your head.
- Don't stop or hesitate as you turn toward the front.
- If you're a beginner, use a wooden pole in place of a weighted bar.

Side Crunch on Roman Chair

(works oblique muscles)

This is an advanced exercise.

Starting Position Climb on the Roman chair, resting on your side. Your top leg extends straight out, ankle under the foot pad. Your bottom leg is forward of your top leg, bottom ankle also under the foot pad. Your legs will be in a scissors-like position.

Movement

A. Inhale as you lower your body slightly.

B. Exhale as you lift your body up as high as you can.

Notes

- Strive for controlled and even movements.
- Don't allow your chest to roll toward the floor or open to the ceiling. Keep your body turned sideways.
- Don't jerk your neck.

Chapter 5

Programs

This chapter contains a variety of complete workout programs. Some are for beginners, some for those with experience. The programs include quick 20-minute workouts, sport-specific training programs, abdominal routines, and other regimens to focus on single muscle groups, comprehensive muscle-building protocols, and examples of circuit and peripheral heart-training workouts.

After trying a few of the appropriate programs for your level of fitness, you will get the feel for how an effective program is put together. At that point, you won't necessarily need to follow any of the specific programs. You'll be able to write up your own programs based on your favorite combinations of the individual exercises, or even design a day's workout in the gym on the spur of the moment. With so many exercises and variations of each exercise, and using the various advanced training techniques described in Chapter 7, the program possibilities are almost infinite. You may find it works best to use some of our program examples as guidelines in designing your workouts, substituting your choice of other exercises as desired for each body part.

However you decide to use this chapter, you'll find that after you've been on a program for a few weeks, you will have to progress it in order to continue getting results. At the end of this chapter, we explain in detail how this is done. We recommend you progress slowly, so as to prevent injury.

By using this book as a reference, you'll have enough information to continue progressing for many years to come, without getting bored—and with continued results.

Remember to make your workouts fun!

Twice-a-Week Training

Here is a sample all-levels program for training two days a week. In this format, you train every major muscle group each time you work out.

Depending on your level of fitness, do either straight sets—3 or 4 sets of 8 to 10 reps—or pyramid sets (see page 139) or some other advanced training method found in Chapter 7. Beginners should start with just one or two sets of each exercise and work with light weights at first. But even beginners should "overload"—use enough weight to really feel it by the last set. Those with more experience should use enough weight to reach muscle failure—the point where they can't complete another rep.

First Workout

Legs
Knee Extension
Leg Curl
Adduction

Chest
Bench Press, Flat Bench
Fly on Incline Bench

Back
Lat Pull-Down
Seated Row

Shoulders
Bar Press (2 sets only)
Lateral Raise (2 sets only)

Biceps
Bar Curl

Triceps
Kickback

Forearms
Reverse Curl

Abs
Tailbone Lift
Crunch

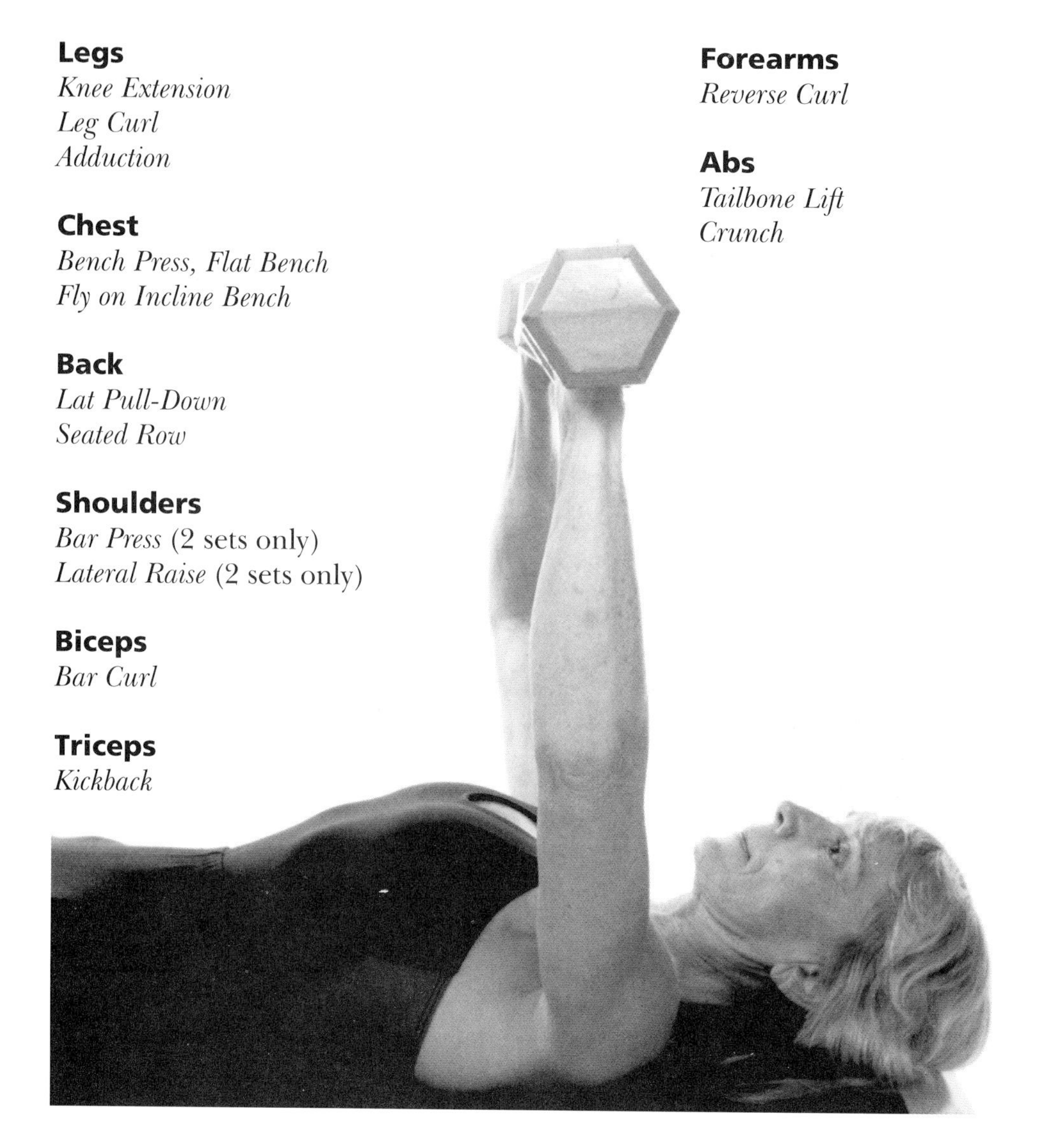

Abs
Pelvic Tilt
Curl-Up—Center

Legs
Hip Extension or Knee Extension
Dip
Squat (2 sets only)
Calf Raise

Chest
Incline Bench Press
Decline Dumbbell Press

Back
Dead Lift
One-Arm Row

Shoulders
Rear Delt Raise (2 sets only)
Front Shoulder Raise (2 sets only)

Biceps
Hammer Curl

Triceps
Reverse-Grip Bench Press

Later in this chapter you'll find sections containing more comprehensive routines for specific muscle groups. To make the above program more challenging, substitute most or all of the exercises listed in those routines.

Twice-a-Week Advanced Workout

First Workout

Legs
Lunge
Leg Curl
Adduction

Chest
Dumbbell Press, Flat Bench
Decline Bar Press

Back
Lat Pull-Down, Back, Close Grip
One-Arm Low-Pulley Cable Row

Shoulders
One-Arm Dumbbell Press on Incline
One-Arm Rear Delt Raise

Biceps
Standard Dumbbell Curl

Triceps
French Press—Black-Eye

Abs
Side Curl-Up
Combined Trunk Curl/Pelvic Tilt

Second Workout

Legs
One-Leg Squat
Knee Extension/Hip Extension
Calf Raise

Chest
Low-Pulley Cable Fly
Pullover

Back
Lat Pull Down, Front, Close Grip
Wide-Grip Seated Low-Pulley Row

Shoulders
Hanging One-Arm Lateral Raise
Front Shoulder Raise with Olympic Plate

Biceps
Hammer Concentration Curl

Triceps
One-Arm Overhead Extension

Abs
Side Crunch on Roman Chair
Knee-Up

Split Routines

Two-Day Split

With a two-day split, you work only half of your muscle groups each day. This means you can safely work out several days in a row without having to take a 48-hour rest between sessions. This format allows for a lot of freedom in scheduling your weekly workouts. You can train three, four, or even five days in a row, take a day off, and pick up again where you left off. The one rule you *must* follow when designing two-day splits is to work opposing muscle groups in successive workouts. You'll achieve greater results by working each major muscle group twice per week. A two-day split makes this possible.

Example 1

Day 1 Legs, Chest, Triceps, Abs
Day 2 Back, Shoulders, Biceps, Abs

Here are programs for all levels of fitness, using a two-day split: Depending on your level of fitness, do either straight sets (3 or 4 sets of 8–10 reps); pyramid sets (see page 139); or use some of the other advanced training methods found in Chapter 7. Beginners should start with just one or two sets of each exercise and work with light weights at first. But even beginners should "overload"—use enough weight so that by the last set they really feel it! Those of you with more experience should use enough weight to reach muscle failure—the point where you can't complete another rep.

Day 1

Legs
Dip (Advanced, do one-leg dips)
Squat (Beginners, omit)
Knee Extension
Leg Curl
Adductors

Chest
Bench Press (Beginners, omit)
Dumbbell Fly on Incline Bench
Pullover
Dumbbell Press on Decline Bench (Beginners, omit)

Triceps
Reverse-Grip Bench Press (Beginners, omit)
Kickback
Overhead Extension (Beginners, use one-arm variation)

Abs
Tailbone Lift (Beginners, use beginning variation)
Crunch (Beginners, use beginning variation)
Side Crunch on Roman Chair (Beginners, omit)
Center Curl-Up (Beginners, omit)

Back

Lat Pull (Beginners, pull to front of body)
Dead Lift, Bent-Knee (Beginners, omit)
One-Arm Row (Advanced, use the bar variation)
Pull-Up (use applicable variations)

Shoulders

Dumbbell Press (Beginners, use beginning variation)
Front Shoulder Raise (Advanced, use internal shoulder rotation)
Rear Delt Raise (Beginners, use incline bench; advanced may perform this exercise standing if they choose)

Biceps

Standard Curl (Advanced, use System 21 training)
Hammer Curl (Advanced, use advanced variation)
Concentration Curl

Abs

Tailbone Lift (use applicable variations)
Bar Twist (use applicable variations)
Crunch (use applicable variations)
Curl-Up (use applicable variations)

Forearms

Reverse Curl
Wrist Curl—Flexion and Extension

Later in this chapter, you'll find sections containing alternate routines for each major muscle group. For variety and a new challenge, substitute those exercises for the ones listed in the above program.

Two-Day Split

Example 2

Day 1 Legs, Back, Biceps, Abs
Day 2 Chest, Shoulders, Triceps, Abs

Day 1

Legs
Knee Extension
Leg Curl/Hip Extension
Step-Up
Squat

Back
Low-Pulley Cable Row
Dead Lift, Straight Leg
Lat Pull-Down
Upright Row

Biceps
EZ Bar Preacher Curl
High-Pulley Cable Curl
One-Arm Hammer Curl on Preacher Bench

Abs
Center Curl-Up
Crunch
Side Curl-Up
Tailbone Lift

Day 2

Chest
Decline Bench Press
Low-Pulley Cable Fly
Incline Dumbbell Press

Shoulders
Lateral Raise
Bar Press
Rear Delt Raise

Triceps
Black-Eye—French Press
Combo Kickback

Forearms
Reverse Curl
Wrist Curl—Flexion and Extension

Abs
Bar Twist (use applicable variation)
Side Crunch on Roman Chair
Knee-Up
Center Curl-Up

Daily (Double) Split

A daily split is when you train two muscle groups in the morning, then return to train two other muscle groups in the afternoon or evening. The major benefit of a daily split is quick results—you can build muscle a lot faster using this format. By training two muscle groups per workout, you're able to focus all your energy on those muscles, which translates into an intense training workload. The downside of daily splits is that they're time-intensive and take a lot of physical and mental energy.

If you're ready for daily splits, you've progressed far enough to choose your own exercises for each muscle group. If you'd like some suggested routines to get you started, turn to the section "Routines for Specific Muscle Groups," which appears later in this chapter (pages 127–128), and plug those routines into the chart.

Example

	Morning	Evening
Day 1	Chest and Triceps	Glutes and Abs
Day 2	Back, Biceps, Abs, and Forearms	Shoulders and Legs
	Day Off	
	Repeat	

Day 1

Morning

Chest
Bench Press on Flat Bench (vary grips)
Incline Dumbbell Fly
Decline Dumbbell Press

Triceps
Dumbbell Black-Eye—French Press
Cable Rope Pull

Evening

Glutes
Squat (multiple sets)
Lunge (multiple sets)

Abs
Tailbone Lift
Center Curl-Up
Crunch

Day 2

Morning

Back
Dead Lift, Bent Knee
Lat Pull-Down (wide grip)
Lat Pull-Down (close grip)

Biceps
Dumbbell Hammer Curl on Preacher Bench
Bicep Curl with EZ Bar (use System 21)

Abs
Side Curl-Up
Combined Trunk Curl/Pelvic Tilt

Forearms
Reverse Curl

Evening

Legs
Knee Extension
Leg Curl
Adduction
Calf Raise

Shoulders
Arnold Press
Lateral Raise
Rear Delt Raise

Cardiovascular Workouts

Peripheral heart training (PHT) and circuit training are very similar. The goal of both systems is to build muscle while simultaneously improving cardiovascular fitness.

PHT involves doing one set of an exercise for the lower body, followed immediately by one set of an exercise for the upper body. There is no rest between sets, and only a very brief pause after the completion of the two sets. You continue this pattern until you've worked all the major muscle groups three to four times.

Circuit workouts involve doing one set of a resistance exercise followed immediately by a one- to two-minute bout of aerobic exercise, usually jogging around a circuit track, hence the name. Again, you continue until you've worked all the major muscle groups three to four times.

Circuit training is recommended for people who want to strengthen their hearts and lose body fat. The intermittent aerobic exercise keeps the heart rate up, which is better for burning fat.

Peripheral heart training does not burn body fat quite as effectively. It is better for exercisers who want to maintain their body composition (fat-to-lean ratio) and strengthen their hearts.

Both systems are equally effective at building muscle.

Circuit Workout 1

Knee Extension: 1/10 (one set of 10 reps), medium weight / 1 minute on treadmill or stationary bicycle

Leg Curl: 1/10, medium weight / 1 minute on treadmill or stationary bicycle

Squat: 1/10, medium weight / 1 minute on treadmill or stationary bicycle

Bench Press: 1/10, medium weight / 1 minute on treadmill or stationary bicycle

Incline Dumbbell Press: 1/10, medium weight / 1 minute on treadmill or stationary bicycle

Lat Pull: 1/10, medium weight / 1 minute on treadmill or stationary bicycle

Dead Lift: 1/10, medium weight / 1 minute on treadmill or stationary bicycle

Shoulder Press with Bar (Variation D): 1/10, medium weight / 1 minute on treadmill or stationary bicycle

Lateral Raise: 1/10, medium weight / 1 minute on treadmill or stationary bicycle

Bar Curl: 1/10, medium weight / 1 minute on treadmill or stationary bicycle

Kickback: 1/10, medium weight / 1 minute on treadmill or stationary bicycle

Repeat whole program once or twice (i.e., do entire circuit 2 or 3 times total).

Circuit Workout 2

Adduction: 1/15, light weight / 1 minute on treadmill or stationary bicycle
Knee Extension: 1/15, light weight /1 minute on treadmill or stationary bicycle
Dip: 1/15, light weight / 1 minute on treadmill or stationary bicycle
Decline Bar Press: 1/15, light weight / 1 minute on treadmill or stationary bicycle
Incline Fly: 1/15, light weight / 1 minute on treadmill or stationary bicycle
Low-Pulley Cable Row: 1/15, light weight / 1 minute on treadmill or stationary bicycle
Bent-Knee Dead Lift: 1/15, light weight / 1 minute on treadmill or stationary bicycle
Arnold Press: 1/15, light weight / 1 minute on treadmill or stationary bicycle
Rear Delt Raise: 1/15, light weight / 1 minute on treadmill or stationary bicycle
Hammer Curl: 1/15, light weight / 1 minute on treadmill or stationary bicycle
Overhead Extension: 1/15, light weight / 1 minute on treadmill or stationary bicycle

Repeat program one to three times (2 to 4 total).

PHT Workout 1

Lunge: 1/8 (one set, 8 reps), medium weight
Dumbbell Chest Press: 1/8, medium weight. Pause if necessary.
Knee Extension: 1/8, medium weight
One-Arm Row: 1/8, medium weight. Pause if necessary.
Calf Raise: 1/8, medium weight
Dumbbell Shoulder Press: 1/8, medium weight. Pause if necessary.
Leg Curl: 1/8, medium weight
Hammer Curl: 1/8, medium weight. Pause if necessary.
Adduction: 1/8, medium weight
Cable Tricep Press: 1/8, medium weight

Repeat three or four times (4 to 5 total).

PHT Workout 2

Step-Up: 1/12, light weight
Bench Press: 1/12, light weight
Dip: 1/12, light weight
Low-Pulley Row: 1/12, light weight
Knee Extension: 1/12, light weight
Lateral Raise: 1/12, light weight
Leg Curl/Hip Extension: 1/12, light weight
Bar Curl: 1/12, light weight
Squat: 1/12, light weight
Kickback: 1/12, light weight

Repeat three or four times (4 to 5 total).

One-Set Weight Training

Most weight-lifting programs use at least three sets of each exercise. However, one-set training—performing just one set of each weight-lifting exercise—can be used beneficially by beginners, elderly persons, those exercising for health reasons only, people with very little time or inclination to exercise, and those who hate to exercise and want to get it over with fast.

Please note that even with one-set training, you can and should do two or three exercises for each different muscle group. Otherwise, your workouts will be much too short, and not very effective! Use enough weight so that your muscles feel fatigued at the end of every set.

For untrained exercisers, performing one set of an exercise builds muscle and increases strength just as effectively as multi-set training—for a while. (Gradually, the benefits will diminish and you'll need to challenge your muscles more in order to progress.) One-set workouts are also good for people who are already conditioned and only want to maintain their current level of fitness. Once you've gotten beyond your first two months or so of weight training, the one-set method won't work if you want to keep improving physically—i.e., develop greater strength and build more muscle, as opposed to just maintaining your current level of fitness. Conditioned exercisers seeking to progress further will require heavier workloads than the one-set training method offers.

One-set training definitely has its place in the fitness arena. Many people who start out with one-set training discover the benefits of weight lifting and graduate to progressive resistance training. Progressive resistance training requires the exerciser to progressively lift heavier weights, to continually do new exercises, and to perform multiple sets of all exercises.

If you have the time and the will, doing three sets is best. But if you are more likely to exercise using one-set training, then by all means do it. Bottom line—any exercise is better by far than no exercise at all.

Following are two sample beginners' programs for one-set training.

Program 1

Legs
1/15 *Dip*
1/15 *Knee Extension*
1/15 *Leg Curl*

Chest
1/12 *Dumbbell Press—Flat Bench*
1/12 *Incline Fly*
1/12 *Low-Pulley Cable Fly*

Back
1/12–15 *Lat Pull—Front*
1/12–15 *Upright Row*
1/12–15 *Seated Row*

Shoulders
1/10 *Bar Press—Front*
1/10 *Lateral Raise*

Biceps
1/15 *Dumbbell Curl*
1/15 *Hammer Curl*
(Select one of the above.)

Triceps
1/15 *Kickback*
1/15 *One-Arm Overhead Extension*
(Select one of the above.)

Program 2

Legs
1/12 *Lunge*
1/12 *Adduction*
1/12 *Leg Dip* (one)

Chest
1/12 *Pullover*
1/12 *Pect Deck*
1/12 *Push-Up* (appropriate level)

Back
1/12 *One-Arm Row*
1/12 *Dead Lift*
1/12 *Lat Pull* (close grip)

Shoulders
1/12 *Front Raise*
1/12 *Overhead Dumbbell Press*

Biceps
1/12 *Bar Curl*

Triceps
1/12 *Black-Eye*

20-Minute Workouts

For those with limited time to train, here are some examples of good workouts for the upper and the lower body that can be completed in a short period. The workouts are arranged for different levels of experience.

Upper-Body Training

Beginning to Intermediate

Chest
Dumbbell Press: 3/10 (3 sets of 10 reps each); overload last set (i.e., use enough weight so that by the last set you really feel it!)

Back
Lat Pull to Front (grip with palms facing toward you)*:* 3/10; overload last set

Shoulders
Dumbbell Overhead Press: 3/10; overload last set

Rear Shoulders
Rear Delt Raise on Incline Bench: 3/10; overload last set

Biceps
Bar Curl: 3/10; overload last set

Triceps
Cable Press: 3/10; overload last set

Intermediate to Advanced (Muscle-Building)

Superset Chest and Triceps

(For supersets, alternate sets of the exercises.)

Bench Press: 4/8 (4 sets, 8 reps per set); overload each set (i.e., use enough weight so that you really feel each set!)

Kickback: 4/8; overload each set

Superset Back and Biceps

Lat Pull Behind Head: 4/8; overload each set

Preacher Curl: System 21; 3 sets of 21, according to the system

Straight Sets Shoulders

Shoulder Press—Variation D (Front or Back Bar): 4/8; overload each set

Lateral Raise: 4/8; overload each set

Advanced

Chest

Bar Press: 4/8 Overload all sets

Back

Low-Pulley Row: 1/8 2/6 1/8 pyramid sets

Shoulders

Dumbbell Press: 1/8 2/6 1/8 pyramid sets

Biceps

Concentration Curl: overload all sets

Triceps

Combination Kickback: overload all sets

Lower-Body Training

Beginning to Intermediate

Knee Extension: 3/10 (3 sets of 10 reps each); overload last set (i.e., use enough weight so that by the last set you really feel it!)

Adduction: 3/10; overload last set

Leg Curl: 3/10; overload last set

Dip: 3/10; each set medium hard

Partial Squat: 3/10; each set medium hard

Intermediate to Advanced (Muscle-Building)

Knee Extension: Drop sets, 1/8 – 1/6 – 2/4

Leg Curl (Advanced variation): 4/8; overload each set; two-second hold at peak contraction

Squat: 4/8; overload each set

Lunge: 4/8; heavy sets

Adduction: 4/8; overload each set; at the end of each set add three partial-range-of-motion reps at peak contraction

Calf Raise: 1/10 each weight distribution

Abdominal Workouts

Here are three sample ab workouts, one for each level of fitness. Ab routines are typically done at either the beginning or end of a training session.

Beginning Ab Workout

Use the beginning variation wherever the exercise descriptions list one. Start with the basic numbers of sets and reps shown below; when you're used to that, follow the instructions under "Progression." When the progressions also become too easy, move up to the Intermediate Ab Workout.

Bar Twist with Wooden Pole: 1/30 (one set of 30 reps). Progression: add 20 twists and use a 10- or 20-pound bar
Tailbone Lift with Knees Bent: 2/10 (two sets of 10). Don't worry about how high you lift your tailbone off the bench; just do the best you can. Progression: 2/15 tailbone lifts
Center Curl-Up: 2/10. Progression: 1/30 center curl-ups
Side Curl-Up: 1/10 each side. Progression: 1/20 side curl-ups, each side
Crunch: 1/15. Knees bent, hands behind head. Progression: 1/30 crunches.

Intermediate Ab Workout

Use the intermediate variation wherever the exercise descriptions list one.

Bar Twist, with 20- or 30-pound bar: 1/50 (one set, 50 reps)
Tailbone Lift to Center: 2 sets to muscle failure
Tailbone Lifts with Torso Twist: 1 set each side, to failure
Crunch: 2/30
Side Crunch on Roman Chair: 1/15 each side
Center Curl-Up, with legs straddled over a bench: 2 sets to failure
Combined Trunk Curl/Pelvic Tilt: 1 set to failure

Advanced Ab Workout

Use the advanced variation wherever the exercise description lists one.

Bar Twist, with 40-pound bar: 1/50 (one set, 50 reps)
Center Tailbone Lift: 3 sets to failure
Tailbone Lift with Torso Twist: 3 sets to failure
Crunch: 2 sets to failure
Center Curl-Up: 2 sets to failure
Side Crunch on Roman Chair: 1/25 each side
Trunk Curl/Pelvic Tilt: 1 set to failure

Routines for Specific Muscle Groups

You can use the following routines to design your own programs. For example, you can adapt them to the formulas for training two times per week, or either of the Split Routines, at the beginning of this chapter. Remember to balance your workouts—work opposing muscle groups equally (e.g., back and chest, biceps and triceps), but not necessarily during the same workout).

The exercises in the Intermediate to Advanced program are more demanding for each major muscle group. Combine the routines for a few different muscle groups, to create your own programs.

BEGINNING TO INTERMEDIATE

Chest

Dumbbell Press on Flat Bench: 3/8-10 (3 sets, 8–10 reps per set); overload last set; i.e., use enough weight so that by the last set you really feel it!
Incline Bar Press: 3/8-10; overload last set
Pect Deck: 3/8-10; overload last set

Back

Lat Pull to Front: 3/8-10; overload last set
Seated Row: 3/8-10; overload last set
Upright Row: 3/8-10; overload last set

Shoulders

Bar Press—Front: 3/8; overload last set
Lateral Raise: 3/8; use a light weight and don't overload the muscle

Biceps

Bar Curl: 3/10; overload last set
Hammer Curl: 3/10; overload last set

Triceps

Cable Press: 3/10; overload last set
One-Arm Overhead Extension: 3/10; use a light weight and don't overload the muscle

Legs

Lunge: 2/15
Knee Extension: 3/10; overload last set
Leg Curl: pyramid using 3 sets
Hip Extension on Knee Extension: 3/12; overload last set
Adduction: 2/15
Calf Raise: 1/15; center weight distribution

Chest

Bench Press: flat bench, standard grip, 4 or 5 sets; overload each set (work the muscle hard)
Bench Press: flat bench, close grip, 4 or 5 sets; overload each set
Decline Press: standard grip, pyramid sets
Incline Fly: pyramid up and drop sets down
Pullover: 4 straight sets; overload each set

Back

Lat Pull to Front: use medium to wide grip; pyramid up and down
Bent-Over One-Arm Row: Pyramid up and down
Seated Row: 4 or 5 straight sets; overload each set
Dead Lift (straight leg): 4 or 5 straight sets; maximum weight possible

Shoulders

Bar Press: pyramid up and down
Lateral Raise: 4 or 5 straight sets (same weight and same number of reps in each set); apply 6 second count
Front Shoulder Raise: 4 sets. Overload each set
Rear Delt Raise: on incline, 4 or 5 straight sets; hold 1 second at peak contraction

Biceps

Preacher Curl: EZ Bar, pyramid up and down
Hammer Curl: System 21, 3 times through; use heaviest weight possible
Cable Curl: 4 or 5 sets, each set to failure; use the heaviest weight possible while still being able to do 6 to 8 reps per set

Triceps

Reverse-Grip Bench Press: 4 or 5 sets, each set to failure
Rope Pull: 4 or 5 sets; maximum weight, with 3 partial-range-of-motion pulses each set
Kickback: drop sets; start with heaviest weight; repeat four times
One-Arm Overhead Extension: 4 or 5 sets; overload each set

Legs

Squat: pyramid sets; do at least 5 sets total
Knee Extension: pyramid sets; do at least 5 sets total
Leg Curl: advanced variation, 4/8; overload each set; take only a 10-second rest between sets
Adduction: 4 sets; go to failure each set
Front Squat: pyramid sets; do at least 5 sets total

Best Exercises for Each Major Muscle Group

Glutes and Legs	Squat
Chest	Bench Press
Back	Lat Pull
Shoulders	Front or Back Bar Press (Shoulder Press, variation D)
Biceps	Preacher Curl
Triceps	Reverse-Grip Bench Press
Abdominals	Crunch and Tailbone Lift

Building Muscle Quickly

Age, gender, training history, fitness level, and previous injuries all will affect your exercise prescription. However, here are some general guidelines for how to get big fast without using steroids:

- To add muscle mass and gain strength and power, you'll have to train hard and heavy. Train with pyramid sets (descending reps, ascending weights), your peak sets being in maximum overload (use a spotter). Over a period of a few weeks, reduce the number of overall reps and make the peak sets even heavier.
- Train each muscle group twice a week, allowing for a 48-hour rest before training that same muscle group again; adequate recovery time is critical to muscle hypertrophy (growth). The only exception is the abdominals, which if you like can be trained on consecutive days. Divide your workouts into daily splits.

Example

	Morning	**Evening**
Day 1	Legs, Abs and Calves	Chest and Triceps
Day 2	Back and Abs	Shoulders, Biceps, and Forearms

- Take one day a week off from all activity. If you have a pool, lake, or ocean available to you, go for a swim a couple of times per week. This will fully relax your hard-working muscles.
- Cut dietary fat to about 10% to 15% of your total daily calories, and eat about 25 grams of protein per day for every kilogram (22 lbs.) of body weight.
- Limit or even eliminate aerobic exercise. Endurance training does not create a physiological environment compatible with rapid muscle growth. If you have a lot of body fat, diet it off as you continue to train heavily.
- Get plenty of sleep. The actual physiological process that increases the size and density of muscle fibers occurs during sleep.
- Finally, stay away from all drugs and alcohol; both interfere with the body's effective use of oxygen.

Without using anabolics, you cannot expect to put on more than three pounds of muscle per month. After a while you'll plateau. (The time frame depends on your individual genetic potential.) From that point on, you can still add muscle, but at a much slower rate—approximately 1% to 3% of your lean body mass per year.

Please be aware that this exercise prescription does absolutely nothing to improve or even maintain cardiovascular fitness. It would be a shame to have worked so hard for such a "buff" body, only to be running to catch a bus and go into cardiac arrest.

Specificity Training for Particular Sports

If you have taken up weight training primarily to improve your skills in a particular sport, you will benefit from specificity training, that is, a weight-lifting program that emphasizes the muscles you use in your primary sport. If your sport is seasonal, these programs are also a great way to keep in shape during the off season.

Specificity training programs are used by competitive athletes to improve their performance, and are not intended to provide a balanced workout. If you participate in a sport recreationally or for aerobic exercise, you may prefer to do just the opposite of specificity training, in order to exercise the muscles that are somewhat neglected by your primary sport. For example, runners and joggers may feel that their legs get plenty of exercise already, and they would be quite justified in choosing one of the workouts emphasizing the upper body.

Here are specificity programs for several popular sports:

Basketball & Volleyball

Back, Shoulders, Triceps: 3 or 4 exercises for each of these muscle groups every workout; do 3 sets of each exercise
Chest, Biceps: 1 exercise each, 3 sets
Abdominals: 3 or 4 exercises
Legs: squats, lunges, and leg curls
Stretching: Stretch every workout; emphasize lower back
Aerobic exercise: At least 5 times per week, 30 minutes or more

Cycling

Legs: 3 or 4 exercises every workout, 3 sets each. Focus on standing exercises. Especially recommended: step-ups.
Upper Body: 1 exercise (3 sets) for each muscle group.
Abdominals: 3 exercises
Stretching: Do not neglect stretching; emphasize hamstrings, quadriceps, and lower back

Running

Abdominals: 3 or 4 exercises
Legs: Do step-ups (3 sets), leg curls, and knee extensions
Chest, Back, Shoulders, Biceps, Triceps: 2 exercises each muscle group, 3 sets each exercise
Stretching: Entire body; emphasize hamstrings and lower back

Soccer

Legs: 3 standing exercises, 3 sets each, and knee extensions and adduction
Abdominals: 3 exercises.
Back, Chest, Shoulders, Triceps, Biceps: 1 exercise each muscle group, 3 sets each exercise
Stretching: Emphasize lower back and legs
Aerobic exercise: 5 times per week or circuit program 3 and aerobic exercise 2 times per week

Swimming

Back, Shoulders, Triceps: 3 exercises each muscle group, 3 sets each exercise
Abdominals: 3 exercises, plus bar twists and side curl-ups
Legs: Lunges or squats (3 sets), adduction (1 set), leg curls, hip extensions (1 set)
Chest, Biceps: 1 exercise each, 3 sets per exercise
Stretching: Light stretching of entire body, emphasizing shoulders
Circuit program: 3 or 4 times per week

Tennis

Abdominals: 3 exercises, including bar twists and side curl-ups
Lower Back: Seated rows plus either dead lifts or straight-leg dead lifts (3 sets each exercise)
Legs: Lunges and step-ups, 3 sets each
Chest, Shoulders, Biceps, Triceps: 1 exercise each muscle group, 3 sets per exercise
Forearms: Reverse curls and wrist curls, 3 sets each
Stretching: Entire body
Aerobic exercise: 5 times per week
Stroke work with 5-lb. dumbbell or cables

Skiing

A specificity training program for downhill or cross-country skiing needs to include components of flexibility, agility, balance, and strength.

To build isometric strength needed for the tuck position in skiing, do some "wall-sitting." Lean against a wall, your legs forming a right angle, as shown in the photograph at right, with your back straight against the wall and your arms dropped. Hold and breathe. Remain in position for as long as you can.

Standard lunges and squats are still the best exercises for building all-around lower-body strength. Crunches, tailbone lifts, and back extensions are essential for building torso strength, which is needed for stabilizing and turning your body.

Hopping from side to side ("plyometrics") will develop power in your legs. Hopping movements closely match the leg action in downhill skiing.

For skiing, lower-body strength is paramount, but strong muscles in your arms, chest, shoulders, and back are also desirable. They help you turn, keep you from tumbling, and in cross-country skiing help push you forward. Bench and shoulder presses, lat pull-downs, bicep curls, and tricep kickbacks target the muscles used in these movements.

Flexibility exercises are important for keeping you limber, so that in case you do fall the likelihood of injury is reduced. Do stretches that focus on full range of motion in all your major joints.

Finally, practice one-legged yoga postures. These will help you develop balance, which is intrinsic to good skiing.

Wall-sitting helps prepare your body for the ski slopes.

Program Progression

Once your body becomes accustomed to an exercise program, it's time to give your muscles new challenges, by changing your program and making it harder. You'll know when this time has come by how your workouts feel. You'll also probably notice that your progress has slowed or maybe even stopped. Hopefully you'll have reached some of your goals by this point in your training—now it's time to set some new ones!

You'll be moving from exercises and movement techniques that are less stressful and physically complex to exercises and movement techniques that are more stressful and physically complex. Be sure to progress in a way that is challenging, but without threat of injury. Following are a number of ways you can progressively make your workout more demanding. These methods guarantee that your workouts will continue to deliver.

Exercise Progression Techniques

- Add resistance (weight). Do everything the same, only increase the workload.
- Use shorter range of motion. See Partial Rep Training.
- Add new exercises.
- Use alternate bars, grips, benches, and equipment.
- Increase the number of sets and/or reps.
- Focus even more on refining exercise performance.
- Keep weights close to the body or over the working muscle.
- Use proper range of motion.
- Apply proper biomechanics.
- Use strict movements when you lift—no jerking, no momentum, no arching the back.
- Use proper foot placement
- Follow appropriate movement patterns, as explained in the description of each exercise.
- Change the combination of muscles worked in the same training session.
- Increase the lever arm of resistance. Straighten out elbows and knees in exercises where they were previously bent. For example, doing lateral raises for the shoulder with arms straight is more challenging than with the elbows bent.
- Take shorter rests between sets. This cuts muscle tissue recovery time. The muscles respond by learning to recover faster.

NOTE: Don't try to incorporate all these techniques at once. Use a few of them each time you feel your workouts need a new challenge.

Chapter 6

Sticking With It

Making exercise an ongoing part of your life—for the rest of your life—will take some planning and effort. Here are some ideas and suggestions that may make it easier for you to stay committed and to exercise for the long run.

First, find a time of day for exercise that you can be consistent with. Pick a time that fits your schedule and lifestyle. Once you have that time in place, be as consistent as possible. But if your schedule must change occasionally, be flexible.

Now and then, take two or three days off from serious exercise.

Recording Progress

When you "train for life" (training to be healthy and fit at all stages of your life), it's imperative to focus on the positive changes, big and small, that occur as a result of exercise. Recording these changes can make them more real and meaningful. Therefore, we recommend you keep a record of your progress as follows:

Heart Rate Note the decrease in your resting heart rate as a result of aerobic exercise.

For three mornings in a row, do the following: Set your alarm at the same time each day. Before even sitting up, find your pulse at your neck or wrist and count how many times it beats in ten seconds, then multiply by six. (For more accurate results, count for 20 seconds and multiply by three.) This number will be your resting heart rate in beats per minute. If the numbers are different each morning, add up the total of all three days and divide by three to get an average. Be sure to have the clock within reach and visible without having to get up to turn on the light.

Blood Pressure Note the decrease in your blood pressure as a result of exercise, and any changes in your eating habits.

You must go to a health practitioner to find out if your blood pressure has decreased. This is well worth the effort. Elevated blood pressure is a risk factor in both heart disease and stroke. Any decrease in your blood pressure means you're lowering your risk of developing both of these diseases.

Joint Flexibility Measure the increase in joint flexibility as a result of the stretching exercises you have been doing.

To discover any increases in the range of motion in your muscles and joints, become aware of how much easier it is to bend, stretch, and reach. Make notations of these increases.

Increasing Strength Record strength increases as a result of weight lifting. Note increased joint stability as well.

To record strength increases, do timed push-ups, curl-ups, and wall sitting. These three tests will give you an idea of the increases in muscle strength in the arms, chest, and shoulders (push-ups); trunk flexors and abdominals (curl-ups); and thigh and buttocks muscles (wall-sitting).

Wall sitting means simply sitting with your back flat against a wall, knees at right angles and feet planted firmly on the floor. The arms hang at your sides. Time yourself and see if you can sit in this position for one minute, then two, etc.

Then, time how many push-ups you can do in one minute and how many curl-ups you can do in one minute. Follow the directions on pages 52–53 and 104 to see how to do these two exercises.

Resting Metabolism Measure the increase in your resting metabolism as a result of weight lifting.

To measure increases in your basal metabolism, you must first buy a digital thermometer. Upon waking, but before getting up, place the digital thermometer under your arm for 10 minutes. The number showing on the digital readout is your basal temperature.

Do this for 4 mornings in a row. Add up the four numbers and divide the total by 4. The result is your basal temperature. If this number is below 96.7 degrees, you probably have a sluggish metabolism. Note the increase in your basal temperature as you become more fit.

Improved BMI Record your improved body-mass index as a result of exercise.

The BMI, or Body Mass Index, is a method of measuring fatness level based on a person's height and weight. Used by both doctors and exercise professionals, it enables individuals to determine if they are at risk for diseases that are weight related, such as heart disease, hypertension, and Type II (Adult Onset) diabetes.

Here is how to calculate your BMI. Multiply your weight in pounds by 700, then divide the result by the square of your height in inches. For example, for a person 5′7″ tall weighing 128 pounds, the calculation would be as follows: 128 lbs. × 700 = 89,600; 5′7″ = 67″ × 67″= 4489. 89,600 ÷ 4489 = BMI of 19.95.

If your final number is above 30, or above 27 with a family history of obesity, then your risk of developing these diseases is moderate to very high. If your final number is 25–27 (with no family history) your risk is low to moderate. If your final number is 25 or less, your risk is very low to low.

In general, a healthy person has a BMI below 25.

Be aware, however, that BMI does not take into account a person's body composition—his or her ratio of fat to lean tissue. Also, it does not consider a person's gender; men are heavier than women and will tend to have a higher BMI without being less healthy. Nevertheless, BMI is well suited for determining risk in sedentary people who have yet to develop much muscle tissue. Body-fat testing is the preferred method for determining risk in athletic and fit individuals.

Fat-to-Lean Ratio Keep track of your improved body composition (fat-to-lean ratio) and your girth measurements. Note how much your physical appearance has improved. To record changes in body composition you must have a percent body fat test done by a fitness professional. The most accurate method for testing percent body fat is hydrostatic, or underwater, weighing. You sit in a tank, up to your neck in water. You're strapped into a chair so you won't float to the top. You then inhale a breath, followed by exhaling as completely as possible all the air from your lungs. While you're holding your exhale, an atten-

Keeping up a training schedule is easier when you can actually see the progress you have made.

dant lowers you, head and all, into the water for 5 seconds. She registers your underwater weight during this time. Very few people get it right the first time, so the test usually takes 45 minutes to an hour to complete. It's an expensive test, around $100, and can only be done in labs and clinics that have the proper apparatus.

Skin-fold caliper testing is also accurate, second only to hydrostatic testing. Armed with calipers, a fitness professional pinches the fat on your body at seven different sites. The seven numbers are then plugged into a formula, and the resulting figures tell you how much body fat you have, compared to lean body tissue. This test only takes a few minutes to do, if performed by a person who knows what he or she is doing. For skin-fold caliper testing to be accurate, you can't take the test right after a workout. Also, you have to be relatively dehydrated (nothing to eat or drink for two hours before the test) and your skin has to be perfectly dry. The tester has to know where and how to pinch you, how to use the calipers, and how to work the formula. Health clubs and gyms usually have staff available to administer skin-fold tests—it shouldn't cost more than $20.

The third method of testing body fat percentage is bioelectrical impedance. You lie on your back, with an electrode attached to your foot and hand. A machine sends a signal from one electrode to the other. The faster the signal travels, the more muscle you have. This is because water conducts electricity and muscle is about 70% water. Fat, on the other hand, is about 7% water, so fat slows down the signal. The test takes just minutes and under ideal conditions is nearly as accurate as caliper testing. The major drawback to this test is, if you're at all dehydrated, the test can overestimate your body fat. To avoid the possibility of dehydration, you're not allowed alcohol or caffeine within 24 hours of the test. Bioelectrical impedance is expensive, around $50. Many health clubs and sports medicine clinics offer the service.

Changes in girth measurements can be recorded in two ways. One, notice if your clothes are fitting you better. Number two, actually take your own measurements. I recommend you measure and record the size of your upper arms (both arms), chest, waist, hips, thighs (both), and calves (both).

Energy Level Note how much more energy you have now, compared to before you started working out.

Keeping track of increased energy is easy. Just feel how much more energy you have for exercise and everyday life.

Setting Goals

Besides being a powerful motivator, keeping records also helps you to set goals for yourself. Having goals in life helps keep life interesting and challenging. The same is true in regard to long-term health and fitness. Set goals that

Keep good workout records to monitor your progress and be able to make proper adjustments in your training program.

can be met by taking small and do-able steps. Have realistic expectations. Don't think you're going to change your body overnight.

Once you've met your current goals, it will be time to set new ones. But let's not overlook the forest for the trees. The process by which we meet our goals is every bit as important and challenging as the goals themselves. The process makes up our day-to-day experiences; it's the "stuff" of life.

Affirm that you're improving in life and you will improve. The power of positive thought is much greater than we can imagine. Turn each negative around into a positive and your life will turn around as well.

A healthy body encourages both a healthy mind and a healthy spirit. When you start taking responsibility for your own health and well-being, life becomes more meaningful and more enjoyable.

Visualization

Visualization can help you clarify your intentions in your own mind, and program your subconscious to help achieve your goals. It enables you to take some control over the "pictures" of reality created by your mind and to direct those pictures in a positive way. This can lead to more control in all areas of your life.

Here is a simple visualization process: Sit quietly with your eyes closed, either cross-legged on the floor or in a chair with your back supported and your feet flat on the floor. Give yourself a minute or two to relax. One effective way to relax is to focus on relaxing each part of your body in turn, starting from your face and gradually working down to your feet. Another way is to breathe deeply and steadily, focusing your attention on your breath as it flows in and out. When you feel relaxed, allow an image to come into your mind's eye of yourself, your body, or your behavior as you would like yourself to be. Make the picture as clear as you can, filling in all the details you can think of. Think of it not as a future ideal but as a present reality. If you like, while holding the image in your mind, you can silently repeat to yourself affirmations, phrased in the present tense, expressing your ideals, e.g., "I am slender and strong," "I have control over how I look," or "I eat foods that nourish and strengthen my body." Invent your own affirmations, ones that feel right for you. Stay with your images for as long as you like, then take some deep breaths and gradually open your eyes. Carry your images with you in your daily life. As you're doing the exercises in this book, you might want to conjure up the body image you've visualized, or as you're shopping for groceries recall your diet visualization.

Trust and believe in yourself. Maintain a positive attitude. What you think directly affects your body; the mind has a great deal of power. Use that power to your benefit!

Make it a practice to take time to visualize.

Chapter 7

Reaching for Higher Levels

Breaking Through Exercise Plateaus

Everyone eventually reaches an "exercise plateau." An exercise plateau occurs when your genetic potential prevents you from progressing any further using the particular exercise routines you've been on. Different people will reach their first plateau at different times, but it usually occurs after about six months of serious training. What you do at that point, to stay motivated and challenged, is a key factor in making exercise part of a long-term healthy lifestyle.

In order to build further strength and develop more muscle, you must seriously increase the training stimulus. The following methods are advanced training techniques and should only be used by those who have utilized all the procedures outlined in the section on program progressions (page 132).

Long-term adherence to exercise and a healthy lifestyle is a dynamic process, ever changing and evolving. So have a flexible attitude. The better quality of life that you experience because of your commitment to exercise will be well worth it.

Advanced Training Techniques

Superset Training Perform two exercises consecutively, in the same or related muscle groups, without resting between sets. After the two sets are completed, you can rest.

Some examples:

- Same muscle group—perform one set of a bench press exercise followed by one set of the incline fly...rest.
- Related muscle group—perform one set of bench presses followed by one set of tricep cable presses...rest.

A lack of rest between sets places a heavy demand on the working muscles.

Push-Pull Supersets Push-pull supersets, such as alternating a set of bench presses with a set of lat pull-downs, is a good alternative to other methods of training. Instead of working the same or related muscles with two exercises, this method works opposing muscles in balance with each other. While one muscle is contracting, the opposing muscle is stretching. This method helps prevent injuries; by working one muscle, you stretch the one you just worked, and vice versa. The stress and strain on each muscle are thereby reduced.

Remember that you need to give each muscle group a 48-hour rest between workouts. If you do push-pull supersets, you'll need to avoid working either the pushing or pulling muscles during that time period.

Pre-Exhaust Training Work a muscle to fatigue as a prime mover (doing your usual number of sets), then do another exercise which works the same muscle as an assisting muscle.

Examples:

- Quadriceps as prime movers: Knee extension
- Quadriceps as assisting muscles: Squat
- Triceps as prime movers: Kickback
- Triceps as assisting muscles: Shoulder press
- Biceps as prime movers: Hammer curl
- Biceps as assisting muscles: Lat pull-down

With this method, the pre-exhausted muscle is worked to maximum fatigue. You can use this technique in combination with other advanced training techniques, such as six-second training, partial rep training, and breakdown training (all discussed below).

Rest-Pause Training Perform one very heavy repetition of an exercise. Then rest (pause) for 10 to 20 seconds. Follow this rest with another rep at a very heavy workload. Repeat 3 to 4 times.

Example:

Do one rep of a heavy squat. Rest 10–20 seconds, then repeat the squat. Repeat this procedure 3 to 4 times.

This method of training requires great effort because during each repetition you're pushing the working muscle right to the edge of failure.

Negative Training A spotter lifts the weight for you, then you slowly lower the weight back to the starting position. The lowering phase of the movement must be slow and controlled, in order for the lift to count.

Example: When doing bench presses—as you hold the barbell, your spotter lifts it for you to the top of the movement, then you slowly lower the bar back down toward your chest.

Because the muscle force is greatest during the lowering phase, a spotter must be used during the lifting phase of the exercise. If not, the person performing the lift won't be able to complete the repetition.

Negative training can be used in conjunction with your regular workouts or with most of the other advanced training techniques discussed in this section.

Negative training is one of the fastest ways to build muscle. However, if you try this method, be careful! Negative training has a high injury potential, because it is during the lowering (eccentric) phase of the lift that injury usually happens.

Six-Second Training An exercise is performed using a 3-second count in both the lifting and lowering phase of the repetition.

Example: Perform a bicep curl taking 3 seconds to complete the range of motion (the lift). Lower the weight, also to a 3-second count. Then immediately repeat.

In six-second training, you're lifting and lowering the weight more slowly than usual. As a result, momentum does not develop and there is continuous tension in the working muscle, which puts extra stress on it.

Whether or not you're using the six-second method, you should always lift and lower the weight slowly and consciously, to minimize the effect of momentum. Using the six-second training method, at least occasionally, will reinforce that feeling of slow, controlled movements.

Partial Rep Training At the end of each set, or at the end of a series of sets, perform 2 to 4 reps using only partial range of motion. The partial-range-of-motion movement is always done at the peak of the muscle's contraction.

Example: Do 3 sets of 8 reps on the knee extension. Then on the fourth set, do 8 reps plus 3 partial reps. For each partial rep, lower the legs about one-fifth of the way down from the peak contraction. (In this case the peak contraction would be when the legs are fully extended.)

Sometimes, but not always, it's necessary to reduce the amount of resistance used in the exercise. Partial rep work is very hard on the joints. Make sure they're sufficiently trained to handle the stress.

System 21 Training The goal of the "21" system, a form of partial rep training, is to combine 3 sets of 7 reps into one intense set of 21 reps. Although the name of the system is based on the number of reps, the way you perform the movements is more important than the total number of reps.

For the first seven reps, lift the weight from the starting position to the midpoint and then lower it. For the next seven reps, start at the midpoint and lift the weight to the top of the movement and back. In the final seven reps, you do seven complete range-of-motion movements.

Example: Do seven reps of a bicep curl, to the midpoint of the curl. Then do seven more reps from the midpoint to the top (peak contraction), then a final 7 reps using full range of motion.

The "21" system can result in faster muscle growth, but it is a very tiring and difficult way to train. Only seasoned lifters should be using this system.

Assisted Training For each set, you begin by lifting the weight yourself as many times as you can until you reach muscle failure. Then, with the help of a spotter, squeeze out 2 to 4 more reps.

Example: Do one set of lat pulls, using relatively heavy weight, until you can do no more; then a spotter assists you through 2 to 4 more repetitions. You must start with a relatively heavy weight or else you'll be doing too many repetitions.

This method of training is very challenging (and beneficial) because you're working to failure with each set.

Break-Down Training Also called drop-set or strip-set training, on the last set of an exercise the resistance used is systematically reduced to permit a few more reps.

A helping hand when you need it or a sharing of techniques are pluses to working out at a gym instead of alone at home.

Example: At the end of your last set of upright rows, work until muscle failure, then put down the bar and reduce the weight from, say, 50 pounds to 45 pounds. Quickly pick up the bar and do as many more reps as you can. Then reduce the weight to 30 pounds to permit a few more reps.

This method of training is very strenuous.

Pyramid Training This method progressively adds resistance, while at the same time reducing the number of repetitions. Ironically, this can also be employed as a beginning method, if you use very light weight and a high rep workload.

Example: Perform 1 set, 8 reps of leg curls at 30 pounds. Next do 6 reps at 50 pounds. Then do 1 or 2 sets of 3 or 4 reps at 70 pounds. You can then stop, or you can reverse the process and go back down in weight for a fourth and fifth set.

This method of training is very time-consuming, but well worth the effort.

Peak-Contraction Training In peak-contraction training, you further flex or squeeze the muscle at the peak contraction (when the greatest number of muscle fibers are involved). Hold, at the peak, for 2 to 4 seconds.

Example: When doing lateral raises, for the deltoid muscles, lift the weights until your elbows are level with your shoulders. Hold and breathe as you flex or squeeze the shoulder muscle for 2 to 4 seconds, then slowly lower your arms back to the starting position.

Avoid the tendency to hyperextend (lock) your joints when holding at the peak contraction. This takes all the stress off the working muscle and can lead to joint injury.

Periodization Periodization is a cyclical system for organizing a weight-training regimen over the long term. It's especially useful for maximizing your performance to coincide with an important game or competition.

The two key elements in periodization are intensity of training (optimal stress) and recovery (complete rest). Both are equally important. A typical cycle lasts two to four months and looks like this:

You train hard for three weeks, then rest

completely for one week. Next, train again at a low intensity for one week, then train hard again for three weeks—only this time make the training even harder than the first three weeks. Then rest completely for a week, and begin the cycle again, training harder each period than the previous one.

Periodization provides an overload that challenges your muscles and promotes optimal response, and it provides recovery time to decrease the potential for injury and allow the muscles to adapt.

If you're training for a competition, time your cycles so that you reach the end of a cycle just as the event begins—you'll be in peak condition at that point.

The slow, stretching movements of Tai Chi provide a relaxing and gentle exercise for those rest days between workouts.

Chapter 8

Flexibility Training

Loosening Up

The primary reason for stretching is to keep your muscles limber, increase joint mobility, and maintain full range of motion in your joints. Stretching also helps reduce muscle soreness and prevents injuries.

Think of your muscles as a willow tree, able to bend in the wind. The more able you are to move and bend freely, the less likely you are to "break" or injure yourself. Weight lifting contracts your muscles; flexibility work keeps them limber and supple. Stretching enhances physical and athletic skills, and aids in the reduction of stress.

The ability to relax your muscles is also very important in developing flexibility. Relaxation is the opposite of tension. Your ability to relax is important because it enhances your ability to decrease tension and its negative consequences. Relaxation is an important part of any stress-reduction program. Also, stretching exercises encourage a union of body, mind, and spirit.

You should stretch after every training session. Of course, you can stretch anytime, but it's essential to do some stretches after every workout. Stretching should be slow and controlled, with no bouncing or pulsing. Push yourself in your stretches. Do stretch to the limit of movement, but not to the point of pain. Breathe deeply and relax into the stretch. Once you've reached your full stretch, hold it for 20 to 30 seconds. As you go in and out of each stretch, be sure to use slow, fluid movements. At the end of the exercise section for each muscle

Stretching is one of the cornerstones to fitness.

group, there are one or two specific stretches pictured for those muscles. These stretches should be performed after training that muscle group.

At the end of each workout, do five more minutes of stretching from the post-workout stretches below. That will be enough to maintain your flexibility, and you'll feel the difference that stretching makes. The benefits of stretching, as with all forms of exercise, are long term. One stretching session will not prepare you for a particular workout.

Torso Stretch

Hold your left wrist with your right hand and bring your arms overhead. Pull your arm to the right as far as you can, allowing your torso to bend but keeping your hips stationary. Repeat to the other side.

Post-Workout Stretches

Inner-Thigh Stretch

Sitting on the floor with your back straight, knees bent, and the soles of your feet together, slide your heels as close to your body as you can. Place your hands on the floor behind your hips and press your knees toward the floor. Hold and breathe for 20 seconds.

Back and Hamstring Stretch

Lie on your back. Extend your right leg. Wrap both hands around your left leg, above the knee, and pull your left leg toward your chest. Hold and breathe for 20 seconds. Repeat with the other leg. This stretch can also be done with both legs at once.

Buttocks Stretch

Sitting on the floor with your legs crossed, lean your elbows either on top of your legs or on the floor, and press forward. Hold and breathe for 20 seconds.

Calf Stretch

With both hands and feet on the floor, walk your hands forward as far as you can, keeping your heels flat on the floor. Don't lock your elbows or knees. Hold and breathe for 20 seconds.

Chapter 9

Workout Accessories

Weight lifting is not an expensive activity. Of course, the biggest expense is joining a gym (or purchasing the equipment you'll need to work out at home). The only other expenses are the purchase of weight-lifting gloves, possibly a weight belt, and later on wrist straps. Special shoes and clothing aren't necessary.

Gloves Weight-lifting gloves provide an element of safety by allowing you to grip the weights better and avoid slippage. They also increase comfort and protect your hands from becoming callused. Weight-lifting gloves are available at the pro shops of gyms, and at sporting goods stores.

Push-Up Bars We recommend using these bars when doing push-ups. They allow you to keep your wrists straight. This takes the strain off your wrists, which should enable you to do more push-ups, more comfortably. Push-up bars are available at most sporting goods stores.

Weight Belt For the average person who goes to a gym to work out, a weight belt is probably not necessary. But if you are a serious weight lifter, and are lifting heavy weights, a weight belt may reduce the risk of lower-back injuries. It also lessens the work of the abdominal muscles and helps to maintain proper standing posture, particularly when performing overhead movements. Most sports shops carry weight-lifting belts.

A weight belt can increase pressure in your abdomen and chest, thus raising your blood pressure. For that reason, don't wear your belt cinched tight throughout the entire workout, but only when necessary for an exercise. Also, be sure to do exercises that strengthen the abdominal and lower-back muscles, so as not to depend solely on your belt for mid-body support.

Wrist Straps These training helps are inexpensive and can also be purchased at gym or sport shops. Their use enables you to lift more weight than your forearm and wrist strength would otherwise allow. It's important, however, to do exercises for the forearm and wrist muscles, and not depend solely on the support of wrist straps. For that reason, we don't recommend the use of wrist straps for anyone until they reach a point in their training when they begin lifting such heavy weights that their forearm strength becomes limiting.

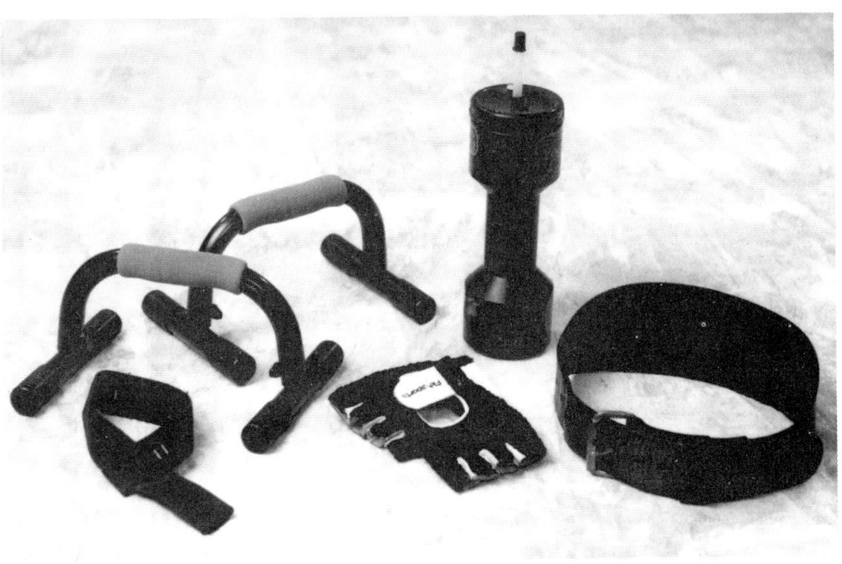

Left to right: wrist strap, push-up bars, glove, water bottle, weight belt.

Chapter 10

A Word of Encouragement

What about those days when you're supposed to work out but are just too tired or not in the mood to do it? Beginners are more likely to feel this way than are those who have been training for a time. That's because regular strength training enhances your energy stores. After a few consistent months on a program, you'll have more energy, not just for your workouts but for all of life's activities. You'll be amazed at how natural, pleasant, and satisfying weight training will feel.

So stick with it. Lifting weights is a lifestyle choice that bears huge rewards. You'll look and feel better, be stronger physically and more self-assured emotionally. Regular exercise will slow the aging process, decrease your risk of disease, strengthen your bones and joints, and boost your self-esteem. In short, exercise improves the quality of your life.

This is the only body we get. By choosing a lifestyle which enhances health and vitality, we're better able to enjoy our lives. So spread the word, not just by word of mouth, but by being a living example. Once you've traveled down the road to health and fitness, there's no going back. Encourage others to join you on your journey!

***Back row:* Anthony, Stephenie, Claudia and Kevin. *Down front:* Jimmy and Lori.**

Name________________________

WORKOUT RECORD

Date	Aerobic	Chest	Back	Shoulders	Arms	Abs	Legs	See Note

Date	Notes

MUSCLE CHART

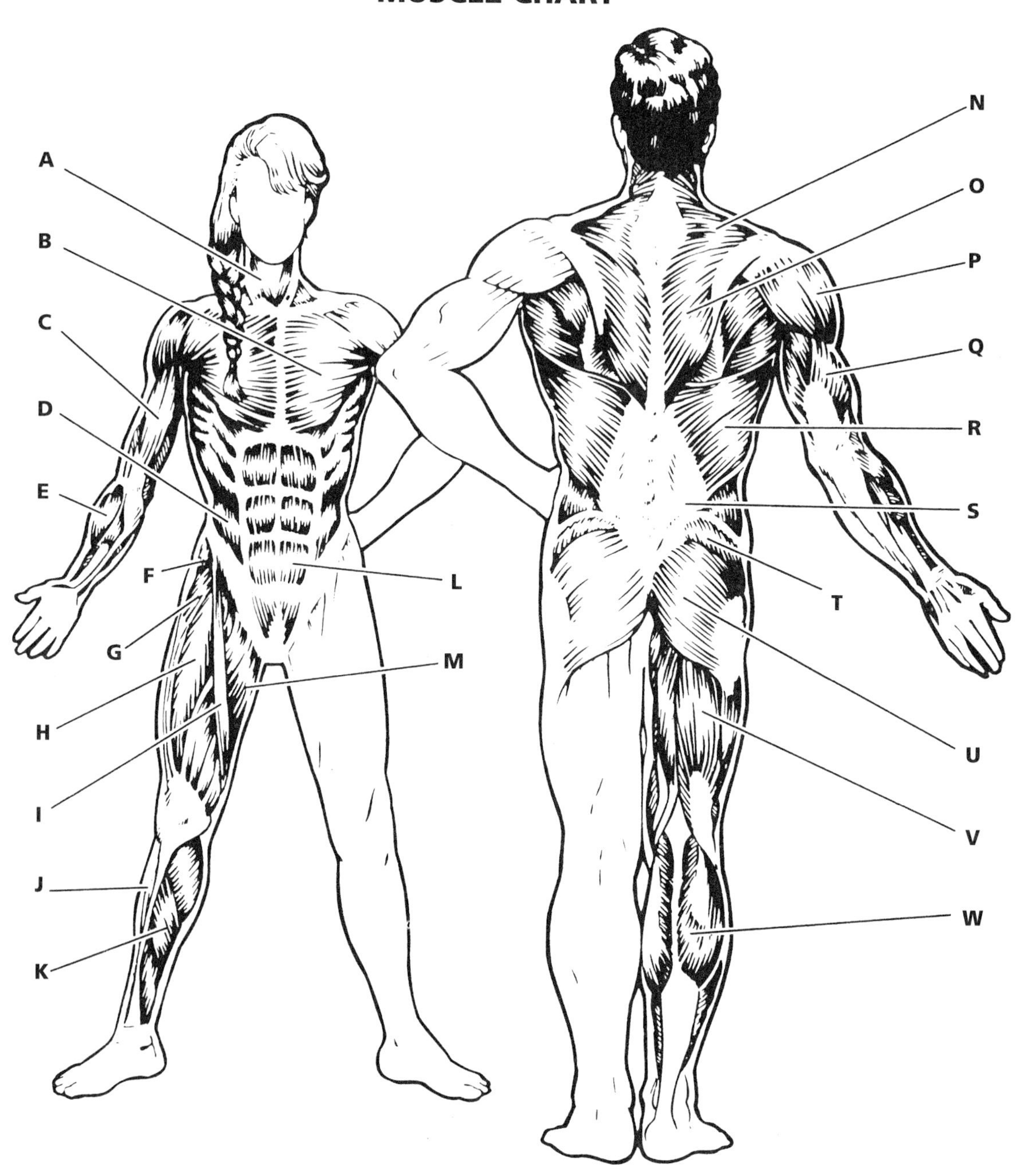

A Sternomastoid (neck)
B Pectoralis Major (chest)
C Biceps (front of arm)
D Obliques (waist)
E Brachioradials (forearm)
F Hip Flexors (upper thigh)
G Abductor (outer thigh)
H Quadriceps (front of thigh)
I Sartorius (front of thigh)
J Tibialis Anterior (front of calf)
K Soleus (back of calf)
L Rectus Abdominus (stomach)
M Adductor (inner thigh)
N Trapezius (upper back)
O Rhomboideus (upper back)
P Deltoid (shoulders)
Q Triceps (back of arm)
R Latissimus Dorsi (mid-back)
S Spinae Erectors (lower back)
T Gluteus Medius (hip)
U Gluteus Maximus (buttocks)
V Hamstring
W Gastrocnemius (back of calf)

Glossary

ABDOMINALS (ABS) The muscles that cover the front of your body from just below the rib cage down to the hip bones.

ACTIVE REST Engaging in alternate exercise which is less intense, allowing your body a chance to recover.

ADDUCTORS Inner thigh muscles.

AEROBIC FITNESS The body's capacity to efficiently deliver oxygen to the muscles so as to sustain vigorous exercise over a period of time.

AGILITY The capacity to change position and direction quickly, with precision and without loss of balance.

ALIGNED POSITION Standing with feet approximately parallel, shoulders and knees relaxed, pelvis tucked, and chin level.

ARTHRITIS A disease which causes inflammation of the joints.

ARTIFICIAL STRENGTH Where you think you're developing strength in one particular muscle, while in reality you're depending on other muscles to assist with an exercise.

ASSISTED TRAINING Training with the help of a spotter.

ASSISTING MUSCLE A muscle which helps the main working muscle or body part to perform correctly.

ATROPHY Muscle shrinkage.

BALANCE The principle of working opposing muscles evenly.

BARBELL A long weight-lifting bar with removable plates, intended for use with both hands.

BICEPS The muscle in the front upper arm.

BMI—BODY MASS INDEX A method of measuring what a person's level of fatness is, based on his or her height and weight.

BODYBUILDING Subdivision of weight training in which the goal is to reshape the body and enhance muscle definition.

BODY COMPOSITION The ratio of body fat to lean body mass.

BODY PART Muscle group; that is, the chest, biceps, back, thighs, etc.

BREAK-DOWN TRAINING On the last set of an exercise, the resistance used is systematically reduced to permit a few more reps.

BURN The sensation caused by products of fatigue that build up in the muscles as a result of vigorous exercise.

CALISTHENICS Exercises that use the weight of the body or its parts as resistance, to increase muscular strength and endurance.

CARBOHYDRATES A primary foodstuff used for energy; carbohydrates are stored as glycogen and transported in the body as glucose.

CARDIOVASCULAR CONDITIONING Training that strengthens and improves the efficiency of the heart, blood vessels, and lungs, and leads to aerobic fitness.

CARRYING ANGLE In bicep exercises, the shoulder, elbow, and wrist are in a plumb line to the floor.

CERVICAL VERTEBRAE Vertebrae in the neck.

CIRCUIT TRAINING Alternating aerobic and resistance exercises to condition both systems.

CONCENTRIC MOVEMENT The part of the weight-lifting movement in which the muscle shortens with tension.

CONNECTIVE TISSUE Ligaments and tendons located in the joints that bind together and support the various structures of the body.

CONTRACTILE PROTEINS Proteins which cause the muscle to contract.

CORONARY ARTERY DISEASE Heart disease.

CROSS-TRAINING Engaging in alternate forms of exercise.

DELTOIDS Shoulder muscles.

DIABETES TYPE II Adult Onset diabetes.

DUMBBELLS Short-handled weight-lifting bars with fixed or removable weights on each end, intended for use with one hand.

ECCENTRIC MOVEMENT The part of the weight-lifting movement in which the muscle lengthens with tension.

ELBOW TENDINITIS Elbow injury from overuse.

ERECTOR SPINAE Inner muscles of the lower back.

EXERCISE PLATEAUS A leveling off that occurs when your genetic potential prevents your progressing any further using the particular exercise routines that you've been on.

EZ CURL BAR Zigzag bar used in bicep and tricep exercises.

FLEXIBILITY Limberness of joints and muscles, measured by the ability to move joints through their full range of motion.

FREE WEIGHTS Barbells and dumbbells.

FUNCTIONAL FITNESS Real-life fitness.

GASTROCNEMIUS The large calf muscle.

GLUCOSE Blood sugar.

GLUTEUS MAXIMUS The large muscle of the buttocks.

GLUTEUS MEDIUS The rear muscle of the upper hip.

HAMSTRINGS The large muscles in the backs of the thighs.

HDLs The *good* cholesterol.

HYPEREXTENSION Locked joint.

HYPERFLEXING Over-stretching a joint.

HYPERTENSION High blood pressure.

IMMUNOGLOBULIN Natural killer cells that protect your body from foreign invaders.

INFRASPINATUS Shoulder girdle muscles.

INSULIN A hormone made by the pancreas.

INSULIN RESISTANCE Insulin is not doing its job properly.

INTERNAL SHOULDER ROTATION Shoulder rotates inward.

ISOLATION Focusing of weight-lifting effort on one muscle or a part of a muscle.

LACTIC ACID A by-product of muscle activity.

LATISSIMUS DORSI (LATS) The primary and largest muscles of the back.

LDLs The *bad* cholesterol.

LIGAMENT The connective tissue that holds one bone to another.

METABOLIC RATE Rate at which your body burns calories.

MITOCHONDRIA The place inside the cell where energy is produced.

MUSCLE FAILURE The state in which a muscle is completely fatigued and cannot perform even one more repetition of an exercise without resting first.

MUSCLE TONE Density (hardness) of muscle tissue.

MUSCULAR ENDURANCE Ability of a muscle or muscle group to exert force over an extended period of time.

MUSCULAR STRENGTH Degree of force that a muscle or muscle group can exert against a resistance.

NEGATIVE TRAINING A spotter lifts the weight, and the person exercising slowly lowers the weight back to the starting position.

NEUTRAL SPINE Straight spine, allowing for the natural curves.

OBLIQUES The muscles on either side of the abdominals; the waistline muscles.

OMEGA 3 FATTY ACIDS Fatty acids which may help to reverse heart disease.

OSTEOPOROSIS Progressive weakening of the bones due to mineral loss.

OVERLOAD Training muscles harder than they're used to.

OVERTRAINING Working out too much for too long without sufficient rest, which can decrease training effectiveness and lead to injuries.

PARTIAL REP TRAINING A method of training where you perform 2 or 3 partial-range-of-motion reps at the end of each rep or set.

PEAK CONTRACTION The point in a lift where the most muscle fiber is engaged.

PECTORALIS MAJOR (PECS) The large muscles of the chest.

PERIODIZATION A method of training which uses a cyclical system for organizing a weight-training regimen over the long term.

PERIPHERAL HEART TRAINING A method of training which builds muscle while simultaneously improving cardiovascular fitness.

PHYTOCHEMICALS A variety of natural compounds that may work to help protect the body from disease.

PREACHER BENCH Slanted bench used in bicep exercises.

PRE-EXHAUST TRAINING A method of training where you work a muscle to fatigue as a prime mover, then do another exercise which works the same muscle as an assisting muscle.

PRIME MOVER Main working muscle.

PROPORTION *See* Symmetry, below.

PROTEIN Compound made up of amino acids, which are responsible for building and repairing the body.

PUSH-PULL SUPERSETS A method of training

which works opposing muscles in balance with each other.

PYRAMIDING A training method in which one performs an exercise with progressively heavier weights and progressively fewer repetitions per set.

QUADRICEPS The large muscles in the front of the thigh.

RANGE OF MOTION (R.O.M.) The range within which a joint can move without hyperextension or hyperflexion.

REPETITIONS (REPS) One complete movement of the dumbbell or body part through the full range of motion.

RESISTANCE TRAINING Working out with weights.

REST–PAUSE TRAINING A method of training where you perform one very heavy rep of an exercise, then rest (pause) for 10 to 20 seconds. This rest is followed by another rep at a very heavy workload. It is repeated 3 to 4 times.

RHOMBOIDS Upper-back muscles.

R.I.C.E. This mnemonic stands for Rest, Ice, Compression, and Elevation; a formula used in the treatment of injuries.

ROMAN CHAIR Gym equipment used for training back and abdominals.

SET A group of repetitions performed without stopping or resting.

SIX-SECOND TRAINING A method of training where an exercise is performed using a 3-second count in both the lifting and lowering phases of the repetition.

SPECIFICITY TRAINING A training program that emphasizes the muscles used in a primary sport.

SPRAIN Over-stretching or tearing of a ligament or the synovial sac which cushions the joint.

STICKING POINT A part of the lift you can't move through.

STRAIN Over-stretching or tearing of a muscle or tendon.

STRENGTH TRAINING Use of variable resistance (weight lifting) to build muscular strength and endurance.

SUPERSETTING Alternating back and forth between two exercises.

SYMMETRY Even development of the muscle groups in relation to each other and the body frame.

SYSTEM 21 A system where you combine 3 sets of 7 partial-range-of-motion reps into one intense set of 21 reps.

T-CELLS Natural killer cells which protect your body from foreign invaders.

TENDON The connective tissue that holds muscle to bone.

TRAPEZIUS The muscle between the shoulders.

TRICEPS The muscle in the back of the upper arm.

TRISETTING Alternately performing sets of three different exercises.

VISUALIZATION Consciously programming the subconscious mind.

WARM-UP The start of a workout; designed

to prepare the body for vigorous exercise.

WEIGHT BELT Thick, strong belt used to support and protect the back while lifting weights.

WEIGHT LIFTING A form of exercise using variable resistance to strengthen, tone, and shape the muscles and body.

WEIGHT TRAINING An exercise program based on weight lifting.

"WORKING THE NEGATIVE" Returning the weight to its starting position with a slow, controlled movement.

WORKOUT As used in this book, a weight-training session.

Index

N

O

P

Q

R

S

About the Authors

Stephenie Karony lives and works in Maui, Hawaii, as a consultant on exercise, nutrition, and lifestyle management. She is a popular lecturer on fitness-related subjects. Stephenie is certified as a personal trainer and a continuing education credit provider for the American Council on Exercise. She teaches applied exercise science, biomechanics, and weight training for the Strong, Stretched and Centered Body/Mind Institute, a school for fitness professionals. Her column "Body Talk" appears in newspapers across the country.

Anthony L. Ranken also lives, works, and works out in Maui. His articles on a variety of topics have been published in several magazines and journals. He is a practicing attorney and co-director of the non-profit organization Maui Tomorrow.

This book follows upon the success of the authors' previous collaborative effort, *Workouts with Weights* (1993), also published by Sterling.